A Day in Our Life

SEÁN O'CROHAN

A Day in Our Life

TRANSLATED FROM THE IRISH
BY TIM ENRIGHT

Oxford   New York
OXFORD UNIVERSITY PRESS
1992

Oxford University Press, Walton Street, Oxford OX2 6DP
Oxford New York Toronto
Delhi Bombay Calcutta Madras Karachi
Petaling Jaya Singapore Hong Kong Tokyo
Nairobi Dar es Salaam Cape Town
Melbourne Auckland
and associated companies in
Berlin Ibadan

Oxford is a trade mark of Oxford University Press

Translation and editorial material © Tim Enright 1992

Irish edition first published 1969 by Government Publications, Dublin
English edition first published 1992

British Library Cataloguing in Publication Data
Data available

Library of Congress Cataloging in Publication Data
O'Crohan, Seán, 1898–1975.
[Lá dár saol. English]
A day in our life / Seán O'Crohan; translated from the Irish by Tim Enright
p. cm.
Translation of: Lá dár saol.
Includes bibliographical references.
1. Blasket Islands (Ireland)—Social life and customs. 2. Kerry
(Ireland)—Social life and customs. I. Title.
DA990.B6502713 1992 941.9'6—dc20 91–25526
ISBN 0–19–212603–2

Typeset by Columns of Reading Ltd.
Printed in Great Britain by
Bookcraft (Bath) Ltd.
Midsomer Norton, Avon

IN MEMORY OF
GEORGE THOMSON
(1903–1987)

ACKNOWLEDGEMENTS

I have to thank my wife Trudy for her help at every stage and Niamh O'Crohan-Laoithe, daughter of Seán O'Crohan, for the front jacket photograph and readily supplying information about the family.

As a result of the work of an active committee *Fondúireacht an Bhlascaoid*, the Blasket Island Foundation, the Great Blasket was declared a National Historic Park by the Irish Government in 1989 and placed under the care of the Board of Public Works. Some of the credit for this must go to Oxford University Press which has kept translations of the Blasket books in print down the years, making them known worldwide. I myself owe a special debt to Nicola Bion of OUP for her active encouragement always; to Angus Phillips for seeing the present book through the press, and to the copy-editor for the care taken with it.

T. E.

CONTENTS

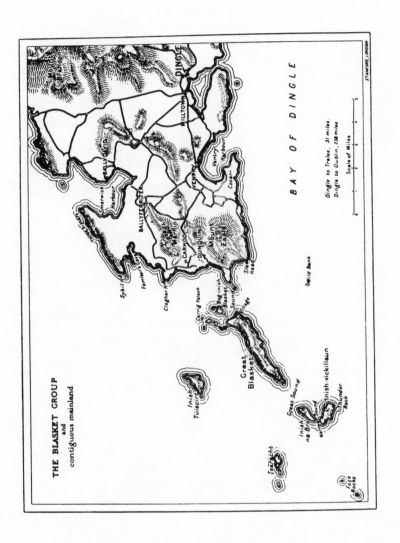

THE BLASKET GROUP
and
contiguous mainland.

BAY OF DINGLE

Dingle to Tralee, 31 miles.
Dingle to Dublin, 236 miles.

Scale of Miles

STANFORD, LONDON.

INTRODUCTION

1

Lá Dár Saol (*A Day in Our Life*), by Seán O'Crohan, is by way of epilogue to the story of the Gaelic-speaking Great Blasket, for it tells how, in its dying days, Islanders resettled on the nearby mainland.

Some ex-Islanders were never able to adapt themselves to life outside their community. One such was Seán O'Crohan's contemporary, Micheál O'Guiheen, last of their poets and story-tellers, who keened over his lost Island all his days. Seán did adapt himself, and to the rapid changes of the twentieth century. He would never forget the Blasket, however, and it is with the critical eye of the Islander that he surveys the mainland scene.

We are told by Jane Austen that 'a removal from one set of people to another, though at a distance of only three miles, will often include a total change of conversation, opinion and idea' (*Persuasion*). Seán's removal to Muiríoch by Smerwick Harbour in 1942 was at a distance of some ten miles, and even though the Gaelic culture was the same, life on the mainland was nevertheless different from that on the Blasket with its small, tightly knit community. He himself gives us some idea of this:

It was seldom now you would hear any of us saying, 'It would be good to be back on the Island.' It was very rarely this tune was heard except when someone would strike up for no other reason than to set someone else going. For, my woe and the sorrows of my heart! We had learnt it was far apart the two places were. That's not to say the

1

Introduction

Blasket would not crop up naturally at other times when we would be reminiscing about the old pursuits and events of our youth. Something that had happened to this one or that. When did Peaid die or Máire Eoin; when did the five asses fall down the cliff? This was only for the crack, if we were short of something to talk about. We did not have that here, for we had no knowledge of the place or what the people were like until we came to settle here.

When Seán was born in 1898 the Great Blasket, three miles off the Kerry coast, was the furthest outpost of western European civilization and virtually unknown. By the time he left it, the Island had become known world-wide through two books, early volumes in a series which has won a special corner for itself in international literature. They were *An tOileánach* (*The Islandman*)* by his father Tomás and *Fiche Blian ag Fás* (*Twenty Years A-Growing*)† by Maurice O'Sullivan which have been translated into other languages besides English.

What makes this series of books unique is that in them we find a community, with its cultural roots in the remote past, describing itself from the inside. E. M. Forster called it 'a neolithic civilisation'. Professor George Thomson, editor and translator of *Twenty Years A-Growing*, described it as a 'pre-capitalist society', and Professor Kenneth Jackson, who published stories he had collected from Peig Sayers, said 'she was like a woman from the Middle Ages'.

Not only was the Island's culture deeply medieval but, when Seán O'Crohan was growing up, the tenants still held their land under the medieval rundale system of scattered unfenced strips in large open fields. He tells us:

Their strips of land were scattered without fences or hedges. The only means they had of identifying their strips were marker stones at the top and bottom, with a couple of beds between the markers. Often

* Oxford, 1951 (translation).
† Oxford, 1957 (translation).

the young lads would come and shift the markers, and often the same rearrangements caused blood to spill.*

Argument over landmarks was ancient and in Deuteronomy we learn that the children of Israel were warned, 'Thou shalt not remove thy neighbour's landmark.' In Homer's *Iliad* we read of 'two men with measures in their hands disputing over boundaries in a common field, contending for equal shares in a small space of ground'.

The land was purchased from the landlord by the Congested Districts Board in 1907 and reallocated in the following years, 'so that every man knows his own plot and has it fenced', as Tomás O'Crohan tells us in *The Islandman*. His book, published in 1929 and immediately recognized as a Gaelic classic, is an account of the old way of life that was passing away. Seán's *A Day in Our Life* came out forty years later and by that time the story-teller was a relic of the past and the public house had become the principal 'gathering house'. The manuscript won a literary prize in 1968 at the Oireachtas, the annual Gaelic festival.

2

By Tomás O'Crohan's day the Irish language had retreated to the western seaboard, except for pockets left here and there. Related to Scottish Gaelic, and at a further remove to Welsh and Breton, it had long been in decline. For centuries it had been conserved by the bards, a highly privileged caste. They received long and rigorous training in special schools where they learned the country's lore, the old sagas which they had to be able to recite, and a variety of highly intricate metres which

* *Leoithne Aniar* (*Westerly Breeze*), (Ballyferriter, 1982).

they employed in the poem-books of their patron kings and chieftains. That old Gaelic order went down in defeat before Elizabethan forces at the Battle of Kinsale in 1601.

Following successive plantations, confiscations, and clearances the clan lands passed to men who were alien in speech, culture, and religion. Gaelic became more and more the language of the dispossessed. The bardic schools had disappeared and the poet's social status sank until the day came when he found his audience in the peasant's cabin instead of his patron's hall. In this way the peasantry, and so the Blasket Islanders, became heirs to some of the rich legacy of the bardic schools.

Daniel Corkery wrote *The Hidden Ireland** to give an account of these later bards whose existence had been ignored by historians of Ireland writing in English. He conjures up a vision for us of 'a motley crowd of Munster peasants of the eighteenth century, gathered into a smoke-filled cabin to hear some wandering schoolmaster or *spailpín*† poet sing'.

It was from that remoter 'Hidden Ireland', the audience of Gaelic-speaking peasantry, that Tomás O'Crohan came. Out of instinct and intuition, and the oral tradition in which he had been reared, he created a literary genre, the collective biography, for *The Islandman* is a picture of his community rather than of himself as an individual. A succession of Blasket writers followed in his footsteps, filling out the picture for us and, to this day, additions continue to be made by ex-Islanders and others to what has become known as 'the Blasket library'.

That the Gaelic language in Ireland has survived the upheavals of the centuries is something of a miracle, and 'the Blasket library' arose out of a set of fortuitous circumstances. The language received its most devastating blow during the

---

* Dublin, 1925.
† Itinerant farm labourer.

years of the Great Famine, 1845–51, when some million people died of starvation along with its attendant diseases, and another million fled the stricken country. Most of these were native speakers and the haemorrhage of emigration continued in the decades that followed, draining them away. By the end of the century the pre-Famine population of perhaps nine million had been halved.

Before the Famine, though Gaelic was spoken in every county in Ireland, English was already the language of pulpit, politics, and the press; the language of upward social mobility. It was taught throughout the national schools system founded in 1831, and it was the language needed by those whose future lay via the emigrant ship. Also, a deadly psychological blow had been given to Gaelic—it became associated in people's minds with the backward conditions out of which the terrible catastrophe of the Famine had arisen.

A change in attitudes began with the founding of the Gaelic League in 1893 to revive the dying language, begin the process of de-Anglicization, and recover Ireland's cultural past. Students of the language soon began to head for the Gaeltacht, Gaelic-speaking districts such as Corcaguiny in West Kerry, and some found their way to the Great Blasket Island.

At the same time scholars were visiting the Island as a result of the founding of the School of Irish Learning in Dublin in 1903. This was a product of the rise of Indo-European philology in the latter half of the nineteenth century when the importance of the Celtic languages was recognized, and of Irish as containing the oldest vernacular literature in Europe. For linguists, folklorists, and medievalists the Great Blasket had a special attraction owing to its remoteness.

A number of students and scholars sat at the feet of Tomás O'Crohan who had learnt English in the Island school but was well into his forties, over half-way through his life, before he acquired the ability to read and write his native tongue; he was largely self-taught.

Tomás was regarded as a master of the language by his fellow Islanders. In the Gaeltacht language is an art form and the best speakers are held in esteem including, as Seán O'Crohan tells us, those whose powers of invective are strongest. The pithy phrase, the quick riposte, the apt quotation from traditional poetry are appreciated and a proverb clinches any argument. *Ni féidir an seanfhocal a shárú*: the proverb cannot be gainsaid. A pupil of Tomás, Robin Flower, the distinguished medievalist who became his close friend and translator, wrote:

This critical alertness is very noticeable in his use of his native language. Those who, like myself, have had the privilege of his friendship and instruction have often wondered at the neatness and precision of his explanations of the meaning of words and phrases, his ready production of synonyms and parallels out of a vast vocabulary, the finish and certainty of his phrasing in ordinary conversation.*

The students and scholars, having made the Islanders aware of the rich cultural heritage they possessed, persuaded them to take to the pen and give a picture of their community to the outside world. Tomás O'Crohan led the way.

3

The Blasket community of subsistence smallholders and fishermen, comprising some 150 souls, was at its height in the years before the First World War, when there was a demand for their fish and it fetched a good price. All this was to change after the war. The Islanders who for so long, and so

* Preface to his translation of *The Islandman*.

successfully, had resisted the old rackrenting landlords, now faced a more daunting enemy, the sealords. Against the giant trawlers which came to scour the seabeds the currach, a canvas-covered canoe manned by three or four men, could not compete. The young began heading for the next parish west, Springfield, Massachusetts. The end was inevitable and it came in 1953 when the last of the Islanders were resettled on the nearby mainland by the Government.

Compounding the decline in the fishing had been the growing reluctance of the younger generation to put up with the lack of amenities which their parents had endured on an island where there was no shop, no doctor or nurse, priest or chapel. I recall Peig Sayers* telling me about her son Micheál O'Guiheen, sitting with a copybook on his knee composing poetry. She regretted it had not been a young woman on his knee instead! Micheál was not the only man of his generation fated to remain a bachelor. Seán O'Crohan, who married Eibhlís O'Sullivan in 1933, was an exception. Eibhlís corresponded for some thirty years, in the English she had learnt at the Island school, with a Londoner, George Chambers, who first visited the Blasket in the summer of 1931 on his way to examine the lighthouse on Tiaracht Island. On 23 February 1936 she wrote to him:

I am the only girl that got married since you were here and I am married three years next May 6th and it was twelve years before that since the last couple were married. Anyway at present nobody thinks of marrying.

Chambers kept the letters and prepared them for publication with an Introduction in which he said of his arrival on the Blasket:†

---

* Married women were commonly referred to by their maiden names.
† *Letters from the Great Blasket* by Eibhlís Ní Shúilleabháin (Cork, 1978).

Introduction

On the afternoon of the first day I was strolling up the hillside when I met two girls coming down with their ass who was loaded with two panniers of turf. Both the girls were bareheaded and wore neither shoes nor stockings and were clothed in little more than rags, but two more beautiful girls I have seldom seen and they were as merry and unaffected with me as though I had been an elder brother; this was my first meeting with Eibhlís and her sister Mary.

In one of her earliest letters to Chambers, 8 September 1931, Eibhlís is already expressing her forebodings:

You would not like to stay here during the winter I am sure. It is a dull place in winter, nothing atall only the pleasant music of the wild seas and the clattering of the wind, but for all I like it anyway, because my dear there is no place like home. My cottage home at the foot of the mountain, and the very day I'll have to leave it won't be a pleasant day for me. I think my dear heart will break that day.

After the birth of her first child she wrote, 28 May 1937:

A cradle in a corner of the house is very strange of course here and strange to all Islanders.

On 27 February 1939 she mused:

Tonight is very fine and the moon is shining bright and I feel a promising of summer in the air and sky. I feel very light hearted about that but such a night in the Island ten years ago when I was just young is very different from this night. There is no stir or sound in this Island tonight, no children laughing or shouting in the moonlight nor later on by this hour when children would be off in their dreams you could hear miles away with the echoes of the strand rows of fair young colleens in four and five in rows after each other singing lovely Irish songs of love and joy and the older folk with their heads out in the open doors gladly listening to them. The Island is just dead I may say but just for old times sake I sang a few verses myself of the old school songs we used have. Pity you were not listening. There was no one but Niamh alone.

Introduction

Three years later, 23 February 1942, the end of her life on the Blasket was at hand:

We have determined at last to leave this lovely Island, I know you will be very sad to hear it, but things are not as they should be and times are changed and expecially for us here with a child at school age and no school and people saying and telling us the child must go to school very soon . . . whatever happens on this Island I have one gifted thing to tell you of it I was always happy there. I was happy among sorrows on this Island.

On the mainland Seán would earn his living as a casual fisherman and from such work as roadmending when that was available. He was recognized as an authority on the West Kerry dialect and contributed to the standard dictionary of the language. He also contributed numerous Gaelic articles to magazines and newspapers for a quarter of a century before he wrote *A Day in Our Life*. The aim of his book, following a short account of the Island's decline, was to give a picture of life on the mainland by means of sketches, anecdotes, and extracts, undated, from letters he had written to his nephew, Pádraig Malone, a superintendent in the Civic Guard in Dublin. He regretted later that some of the pieces in his book were so short.

As Seán's main concern was with life on the mainland, he does not tell us, for example, about the seven weeks he spent in England in 1952 where he worked as a porter at New Street Station, Birmingham. His friend, the late George Thomson, was Professor of Greek at the university in that city and Mrs Katharine Thomson recalls Seán saying how bewildered he was at first by the crowds pouring into the station, reminding him of the seagulls flocking on to the Island. She also remembers him step-dancing in their home. He tells us in his book about his love of dancing and he was indeed a fine step-dancer, as I can myself attest. His father had been a good

9

dancer and so had his father before him. And like so many others on the Blasket he was a musician too, playing the fiddle and the melodeon.

From the Blasket he brought with him the independence of mind that was native to the Islander. He tells us:

The Government of England ruled this country but in those days the Islanders did not know what a government or state was ... What we had on the Island was for all the world self-government. If you did anything wrong, or acted in an unacceptable way, the people there would not be content to let it pass. You had to keep to the straight path always for, if you did not, the Islanders would step in and correct you.*

His father had written:

Talk was beginning throughout Ireland about winning self-government, or Home Rule as it is called in another language. It was often I told the fishermen at this time that Home Rule had come to the Irish without their knowing it and the Blasket was where it had begun ... We had characters of our own each different from the other, and all different from the mainlanders.†

It is not surprising that the community values of the Great Blasket should appear so attractive to those brought up in the acquisitive society of today. They 'lived in the shadow of one another', as they said of themselves. The Islander derived his quiet self-confidence, his dignity, and courtesy from a lively awareness that he belonged to a community where all were equal; where man was not only at one with himself but at home in his natural world along with his fellow creatures of land and sea; where story-telling made the past part of the living present and the wisdom of the ages was learnt round the hearth. Micheál O'Guiheen 'The Poet' said that his mother, Peig Sayers, spoke virtually in proverbs, and not only do we find

---

* *Leoithne Aniar (Westerly Breeze).*
† *The Islandman.*

proverbs quoted everywhere in the Blasket books, but we find them rephrased and embedded in everyday speech.

4

Three Islanders who grew up together have left us a triptych depicting the Blasket from its glory days to its abandonment and the aftermath. In *Twenty Years A-Growing* Maurice O'Sullivan wrote of idyllic childhood and youth. In *A Pity Youth Does Not Last** Micheál O'Guiheen 'The Poet' mourned the Island's decline, and Seán O'Crohan's *A Day in Our Life* tells of Islanders in exile, which for them it was, even when they could see the Blasket every day of their lives from their mainland homes.

Maurice O'Sullivan's style is lyrical and spontaneous as he recalls boyhood wonders on his magic island at the rim of the western world. The style of Micheál O'Guiheen is that of his mother Peig Sayers, whose scribe he was for *Peig*† and *Machtnamh Sean-Mhná (An Old Woman's Reflections)*.‡ Peig was unlettered and the rich music of her prose flows from the mouth of the traditional story-teller. Hers are Homer's *epea pteroenta* 'winged words', in that they fly from mouth to ear. The Blasket writers made the printed page talk.

Seán O'Crohan's is a robust and racy language, reflecting his sanguine outlook. It has the vividness and immediacy which derived from the oral tradition out of which he came. Story-telling was no passive recitation of tales, often well known, but a re-creation. It was communal rite, the audience responding with laughter and groans to the modulations of voice, the mobile face, and the hand gestures of the story-teller, who

---

* Oxford, 1982 (translation).
† Dublin, 1974 (translation).
‡ Oxford, 1962 (translation).

would be inspired in turn to rise to new heights, the well-rounded phrase and the image freshly minted evoking murmurs of appreciation.

Seán, nurtured in this ancient art, brings flesh and blood people before us with conversational ease and rollicking humour. Tomás had cast a mildly ironical eye at his fellow Islanders and chuckled at their foibles in his first book *Allagar na hInise* (*Island Cross-Talk*) (1928).* It is what Seán does on the mainland, only the irony is sharper and the laughter louder. Nor does he spare his tongue on clergy or nuns, something that would be outside the norms of Irish writing in English but was firmly within the Gaelic tradition, as for example in Eoghan Rua O'Sullivan, the eighteenth-century poet whom he quotes. Speech in the Gaeltacht was always forthright while at the same time delighting in tongue-in-cheek exaggeration.

For Tomás O'Crohan, who was born and died in the Blasket, and who never travelled far from it, the mainland was where the Islanders might find marriage partners. There was a saying, 'Marry an Islandwoman and you marry all the Island.' On the mainland they got married and were baptized; sold their fish, sheep, and rabbitskins; purchased their goods and took the opportunity of having a drink, and the inevitable session of song, saying 'This is a day in our life.'

Seán, with his sketches of life on the mainland written at times with ribald gusto, complements his father's more restrained account of life on the Blasket so that, together, they provide a rounded picture for us of the West Kerry Gaeltacht.

Eibhlís, Seán O'Crohan's wife, died aged 60 in 1971. Seán wrote another book shortly before he died aged 77 in 1975, following an accident in which he was knocked down by a motor-vehicle while walking near his home. This second book

---

* Oxford, 1986 (translation).

was a compilation of Blasket lore, and it was published in a volume entitled *Leoithne Aniar* (*Westerly Breeze*), which also contains interviews with Seán and others about life on the Blasket.*

So, in the last months of his life the thoughts of Seán O'Crohan were back on the Island of his youth, now long abandoned. In the school there he had taken his first steps as a writer, for in his day, unlike that of his father, pupils were taught to read and write their native tongue; they were also encouraged to compose pieces for Gaelic journals. A story of his in the Tralee Gaelic League monthly *An Lóchrann* (*The Torch*) brought a note from the editor telling him his writing had 'power and polish'.†

In *The Islandman* Tomás O'Crohan had recounted the old heroic life on his remote Island for, as he says, 'the like of us will never be again'. There is no sentimentality in his gritty prose which reflects a man who has accepted stoically the hardships of life in a place where, for example, the people might be stormbound for weeks on end. The ancient Greeks taught us to look at the world without illusion and self-pity; in Homer man rises without despairing to meet the challenges and suffering which are his lot. That is the very spirit of Tomás, whose wife and eight of their ten children had died at various ages by the time he was writing *The Islandman*. He passed on that spirit, along with an incomparable legacy of language and lore, to his youngest son Seán, who lived with him until he died in 1937. In Seán we find no trace of sentimentality either, despite Matthew Arnold telling us that 'sentimentality, if the Celtic nature is to be characterised by a single term, is the best term to take.'‡

---

* *Cló Dhuibhne* (Ballyferriter, 1982).
† *Oidhreacht an Bhlascaoid* (*The Blasket Heritage*) (Dublin, 1989).
‡ *On the Study of Celtic Literature.*

Introduction

A Day in Our Life mainly depicts the old Gaelic world of West Kerry caught up in the rapid changes which the second half of the twentieth century has brought. The subject of *Westerly Breeze*, as its editor Pádraig Tyers tells us in his Introduction, 'is the Blasket and the spirited, grand people that lived there'. Seán's second book has the same racy style as the first, and we are not surprised to find a glint of humour in his eye as he recounts the lore of the Islanders. His was no 'Island of saints and scholars' but a place where ordinary people lived, over whose warts he felt no need to apply a coat of whitewash.

Seán O'Crohan was a realist and an optimist with one leg in the new world, while the other was firmly planted in the old, for he could never forget the Great Blasket. As he tells us in the very last sentence he wrote: 'I saw with my own eyes on the Western Island the finest life I would ever see.'

T. E.

'Yerra, wisha, this is a day in our life, and we shall not always be in the way of a day like it.'

Tomás O'Crohan, *The Islandman*

Morning

Morning

ꙗ

Signs appear of what lies ahead but, if so, small is the notice taken until it comes to pass. That is how it was with us and we living on the Western Island. We were young and strong with little sense or wit, the case ever with young people before life sharpens their notions for them.

It is well I remember the day when Pádraig Kearney left the Island along with his wife and family. They went to settle in a poor bare hovel in the glen of Clochán Dubh, where they had neither holding nor living and could only depend upon the help of God. But Kearney was not long gone from us when no one was giving him any thought at all, and the Islanders were ploughing on. He had given away the holding he left behind and a blessing from God this was for the man that received the gift.

People were marrying on the Island the same as ever and why wouldn't they? Isn't it there the best living in Ireland was to be found: potatoes and fish fresh and salt, Indian meal and flour, tea and sugar. If there was hunger anywhere, you can rest assured it was not on the Western Island.

Here is another thing: when the eldest son came to marrying age he would have to clear out of the house if he refused the hand of the woman his father found for him. The second son would take her for his wife instead. There was no such thing in those days as 'put your hand under her oxter and carry her off with you'. It was a case of the wife your father found for you, or no wife at all.

The eldest son would marry surely and, after he had lived for a year or two with his father and a couple of brothers, a new house would be built for him and his wife. The second son would marry then in the old home and in due time he would have a new house built too, leaving the old home to the youngest son.

These used to be known as the 'flower of the Island' and they were the men who took the lead in everything there.

But, talking of signs, didn't Seán Mhuiris and his wife leave us, and nobody expecting it at all; they made for the Parish of Ventry where they settled. The biggest wonder was that Seán Mhuiris was one of the leading men, so there was the world of talk over him and his wife going. People saw it as the start of an epidemic, for rumour had it that Lítheach was looking out for a place on the mainland too and Lítheach was Seán's own brother.

Howsoever, if some people were leaving the Island, others were staying put and setting up home there. It had a school with two teachers in those days and around fifty scholars in attendance. Some people were marrying while others were scattering east and west, emigrating overseas as soon as they were old enough.

We knew neither want nor any scarcity except that we had to put up with the winter and bad weather; diseases too and sicknesses that affect such a place, with no remedy or cure to hand. An Islandman needed courage above all, but the time would come when that would fail you there.

An old man died and his house was left falling to ruin with nobody to take it over. A man with six in the family took sick and it came as a great blow to the rest of us when he died. His wife had married in from the mainland and, within a year from that day, she and her flock were gone from the Island; another house left falling to ruin. There were as many as five of these now, all within the space of nine years.

The Islanders were rowing away with a will and a drive yet. Still and all they had lost the lively spirit they had in them in years gone by. Some would have it that the vim and vigour were dying out of the Island. As one member of a family crossed over to America he would be laying the passage money by for the next brother or sister back home to follow in their turn.

Before long the effects of all this were making themselves felt. An elderly couple had a young son at home with them still and they doing fine, for they had eight of the family over in America who never slackened in posting money home. Death swept away the young boy with an incurable disease. This left little courage in anyone and the Island was under a cloud of sorrow for a good while afterwards. The day came when the old couple said goodbye and farewell, and it would move a heart of stone to be looking at the two of them parting from the place of their birth.

All the children of another couple had emigrated across the sea and they were pressing the father and mother to find some cabin for themselves on the mainland where they could spend the latter end of their days. The time came when they also took their departure and said goodbye to their native place.

That was how the signs were making themselves plain to us for long enough. All the same there were many who paid little heed to these happenings, since they had the life to suit themselves still, and were thriving. Visitors galore used to be coming in and there were those among them who thought Paradise could not better the Blasket. That was no wonder; wasn't it they had the easy life of it there with little strain or stress. It was the natural courtesy of the Islanders that won the hearts of the visitors and it was no word of a lie for the person who wrote at this time: 'You would leave it for no other place but the Paradise of the Blessed Saints.'

This was the time when the Island was at its height but by the same token it was at this very time that the storm was waiting to blow. We were getting on with our lives, making the most of what opportunities came our way. There were young women there still and they ready to leave home any day. When you reach a certain age a fondness for the women takes hold of you and, if you find a willing partner, not even bullets will hold you back. You do not look ahead at all and devil the better for it you would be if you did.

As the luck of the devil had it, I met a young woman and if I did I let no one else have her but myself. I went up to Ballyferriter* with her and we were joined together with a couple of words, and that was that. According to some it was the height of bravery, while others thought it was madness to marry on a rock out in the sea, when married folk who had spent their lives there were leaving it or had gone already.

I had nobody at home before herself only my father, and he was the happy man surely that we had a woman around the house once again, for we were in need of her for many a long year. We were short of nothing in the world. My father hadn't a hand's turn to do except bring a load of turf down from the hill, and that was only if he felt so inclined. He was his own master, but all he ever wanted was hill and strand. We were on the pig's back. 'The whiter the cloth the easier it is to stain', however, and before a year was out my father got a stroke that left him without the use of hand or foot. During the next couple of years he would be sitting up for one while and lying down then for another while. The age was there of course and

---

* On the mainland, where the parish priest lived and marriages took place.

no improvement in store for him, so the day came when he said goodbye to the troubles of this world.*

Visitors galore were calling to the house now, waving *An tOileánach*† and *Allagar na hInise*‡ in their fists. They put us off our day's work as they roamed in and out wanting to see the house where the hero was born. That was the way of it year after year.

But the day came when the people who used to keep visitors had departed from the Island and finally there was only one house left in the village suitable for lodging them. The day came too when the rest of us received another jolt: a man with his wife and family of four cleared off to the mainland. We had a young baby ourselves by this time and the position we were in was dawning on us. There was our little child; what if she took sick? What could we do for her with no doctor or nurse on the Island?

The Islanders were ploughing away, some struggling to make ends meet, while others had full and plenty, the same as you find everywhere. One evening the story ran round the village that a youth of twenty-one years had fallen down a cliff.§ Pulling furze for kindling he was when his footing gave way and down with him until he hit the sea. There was no life or soul in the Island for a long while afterwards.

Early one morning a man came to the door to say that his old father had been ailing for days and was asking for the priest. No man fit enough to do what was needed could refuse in such a case; he had to bestir himself. Three miles of sea to be

---

* Thomás O'Crohan died aged 81 on 7 March 1937.
† By Tomás O'Crohan (Dublin, 1929), and in translation as *The Islandman* (Oxford, 1951).
‡ By Tomás O'Crohan (Dublin, 1928), and in translation as *Island Cross-Talk* (Oxford, 1986).
§ Tomás, son of Peig Sayers, for whom his brother Micheál 'The Poet' wrote a long lament.

crossed and recrossed with the priest, who had to be taken back out again. There was the return journey then, in all twelve miles of sea and wind and tide.

To be fetching in priests and doctors for poor creatures in their hour of need was another cloud hanging over the Island, and we all trying to lend a helping hand to one another.

The young were scattering east and west now, the parents falling into age and their families parting from them, although this was with no great eagerness or lightness of spirit. The population was going downhill fast and the Island was failing. Another couple left that had a family of seven children big and little. The day of reckoning came for the two teachers and one of them had to depart. There were no longer enough scholars for two and small hope that there would be ever again. Even the day came when the remaining teacher had to take her leave. The number of scholars had dwindled to five, so the school could be kept open no longer.

It was another sign that matters were coming to a head. The Islanders were churning these events over and over saying, one after another, that the vessel was sinking and the man who jumped overboard first would be the best off.

Our own child was about six months old by this time. One night she was bright and lively with nothing whatever ailing her and we going to bed, but in the middle of the night she sickened and it began to look serious. We spent the rest of the night watching over her and all next day as well. There was nothing we could do for her because the sea was too high and the wind too strong. However, on the day following the wind abated a little and we made a run over to Dunquin. It was the district nurse we brought back with us, for the whole day might be gone before we could get hold of the doctor. After the nurse had seen to the baby we rowed her back out and that was that.

Morning

This is how things were fretting us and, when you have a child of your own you have pity in your heart for the creature, and want all to be for the best. A while after this the woman of the house took sick suddenly in the middle of the night. I called in an old woman from the village who was well versed in women's ailments and nothing would make her easy but to have the doctor fetched across.

I had to set off at that hour of the night and muster three men to row out to Dunquin with me. I had to knock up the driver of the hire-car and head for Dingle to fetch the doctor back with us. The doctor brought my wife through the danger and we had him back over in Dunquin once more before there was any glimmer of day yet.

Another morning, a while afterwards, a man called to the house saying, 'My cow is in heat and I must take her over to the mainland to the bull.' This caused me no great qualms for I was an old hand at coping with that kind of rough and tumble. Two currachs were made ready with eight men, each man knowing his own task. The cow has to be heaved over on to her side on the slipway. Her legs are spancelled and she is lifted into the currach. The rowing is done by two men at the prow and another at the stern, unless the wind is fair for hoisting the sail.*

The currach is brought in alongside the landing stage at Dunquin Harbour and the cow is lifted out by dint of main strength. The spancels are removed and she is let go where her instinct leads her. She is brought back home again in the same way and left in a shed until morning. That, I'm telling you, is the hard-earned drop of whitening for the tea, as a man who watched the performance was heard to say.

A man and his two daughters were the next to leave us. His

---

* The second currach followed the first in case of accident during the crossing.

house was up for sale and nobody ready to offer a halfpenny for it, a span new house with good timber in the roof. A relation of his approached myself to see if I would be willing to pay something for it, since the man was leaving penniless. I reckoned it was a far better house than my own and furthermore it might come in useful yet if God spared me. I bought the house, paid for it, and a happy man he was to have the few pounds in his pocket going away.

Soon after this my wife's sister married over on the mainland and from that day onwards herself was unsettled on the Island. Then again the child was a cause of anxiety to us with no schooling or proper upbringing in store for her. It was a load on the mother's mind on top of worries she had about herself. The signs were coming thick and fast now: people leaving and the man behind waiting only for his own turn to be off. But what did we know about any other place or how to make a living there? That was the only consideration holding us back now.

One day I was sitting on top of the hill above the village smoking my pipe for myself. I had sent the cows up Mám Chlaointín and was pondering about the people who had left the mark of their toil on the big bank-walls and heavy stones, the large broad ridges, those great works lying there before my eyes. Says I to myself, 'Not a single descendant is left on the Island today of the folk that left these remains behind. There can be no doubt but there were people here hundreds of years ago.'

These thoughts were going through my mind and it struck me that the original inhabitants had either abandoned the Island or been driven out of it. Nobody has any tidings of them now but they left their mark behind and there it will remain so long as the Island itself remains above water.

I gazed down towards the village. It was there below me like the nest of a hen that you might happen upon with all her eggs lying neatly together. I began counting the houses and when I had made a tally of those that were empty I could scarcely believe it. Twelve there were, all now deserted. I said a prayer for the souls of all the dead.

Herself and myself were sitting by the fire one night. The wind was blowing outside and the rain lashing down. It was a black and threatening night. She had paid a visit over to the mainland by this time along with the child. She said that, judging by the comfortable life of it people had outside, it was in a grave the Islanders were living. On and on she went about life on the mainland, the peace and ease people had there with no swell or surge of the sea washing over their rock. Even if they had some small needs they were far better off than to have full and plenty in this place, where disaster was waiting to strike from night till morning.

'This is the last winter here for me,' she declared, 'and for the child, make no mistake at all about that, even if I have to shoulder my own pack! Other folk are leaving here, unlike me, and by the boatful. There's no fear or mad fright on them either, the same as there is on the rest of ye, that the devil wouldn't shift ye out of here . . .'

That was the sermon she gave me and it wasn't in Latin either, with every word of it sinking home.

'Yes, girl,' says I under my breath, 'you will leave here and it will be a death sentence for me.'

But, when your wife is called Eibhlís (Elizabeth) and the 'Queen', you may as well pull off your trousers, draw them high up over her backside and let her rule the roost. I prayed for the help of God and the Virgin Mary that whatever was in store for us would come from their hands, for any day you place yourself under their protection you will not go far astray.

Another bad night came when the wind was blowing from

the south-east and a gust struck the side of the old house sweeping all the eaves away. A second one would have left us clean without a roof over our heads. That gust of wind gave the 'Queen' her text for another sermon. It settled the matter and I made my mind up that another winter would not catch me there.

I set off for the mainland one Sunday, telling herself that I intended to pay a call on my uncle and aunt north at Muiríoch. All they had was a house at the side of the road, no different from our own, and the long broad bay of Smerwick Harbour for fishing. Eibhlís warned me not to come back home without finding some site for a house up there, or it would be the worse for me.

Some old cabin was what I wanted if I could find one. It would be easy for me to build on to, for I had the other house on the Island with the good new timber. It was with no great eagerness I crossed the Sound, but no great reluctance either.

I strolled in the door to my uncle and aunt at Muiríoch and they not expecting me at all. By the same token neither of them asked what brought me but left it for myself to say. I told them and, if I did, for me there was the welcome. They found me a house straight away and I had wings on me going home. The 'Queen' sprouted bigger wings still when she heard the good news.

Within a couple of days two strong hardy lads and myself were up on the roof of the house I had bought two years before, and by evening we had gathered everything together. We came next day and hauled the timber down to the Island harbour. The day after that we ferried it across to the mainland in two currachs full to the brim. A lorry from Dingle hauled it north to Muiríoch.

We had the bulk of the work done now, except for our cow and a year-old heifer. The neighbours helped us to ferry them over to the mainland and a Dingle man bought them. Small light articles were all that remained.

Between times Peig Sayers and her son 'The Poet'* had gone out to settle in Dunquin. It brought it home to me then that the Island's day was done and soon it would be a vessel sunk in the middle of the ocean.

News came south to us that possession of the house had been taken, the lock was on the door and the key at my uncle's. In June 1942 Eibhlís went out to stay at her sister's house with the little girl, saying goodbye and farewell to her people on the Island.

I was sending my bits and pieces over to Dunquin at my ease where it would be no trouble to me to pick them up after I had settled in above at Muiríoch. It was the end of summer by now and I was getting impatient for news that all was ready for us to move in. The war had been going on for a couple of years and things were growing scarce. I stored away a couple of half-sacks of flour in a safe nook in Dingle, two items that were to prove the greatest boon to me afterwards. We had tea and sugar to spare because we used to bring tea back to the Blasket in pounds, and sugar by the stone weight.

One morning, when the sun was up, the wife's brother called to the house saying, 'If you have any thoughts of going north by sea, this is the day for it because wind and tide are in your favour.'

It was just what I wanted to hear. We gathered whatever was left and all the Islanders came to help us load the currach. We pulled away from the harbour, heading northwards towards Eireaball and from there on to Fiach off Sybil Point, north-east then past Béidrí mouth. We reached the Submerged Rocks and

---

* Micheál O'Guiheen, last of the Island's poets and story-tellers, author of *Is Truagh Ná Fanann an Óige* (Dublin, 1953), translated as *A Pity Youth Does Not Last* (Oxford, 1982).

carried on round Carrigbrean until we pulled in at Ballydavid Quay.

That is about twenty miles of sea in all, with only two of us manning the currach and it laden from stem to stern with household goods. The weather on the day was as glorious as anything that has come since. There are few who would not have been moved to tears by the peace and quiet on the sea. This is how it affected me, and the man who was with me too.

A fine hefty man came along with a welcome and twenty for us. We threw the mooring rope up to him and he brought his horse and cart alongside. In no time at all he had all our goods carted off to Muiríoch for us.

Everything was brought to the door of our new home and it lifted my heart to see smoke rising from the chimney. Eibhlís and the little girl were there before me, and several people from the village had gathered to welcome us too, some of them our own relations. All was put away in its own place without hurry or fuss. We were at our ease for the first time in many a long day, and in our own small comfortable house on the mainland.

Midday

Midday

𝛅

*T*he first of September is here and there is nothing to say in its favour. We had very bad weather last night. It could not have been worse if it had been St Brigid's night, the first of February.

The poor farmers are in a sorry state over this same weather and with good reason. All the people's talk is of the weather and what has happened to it in recent years. As they say themselves, there's no use harking back to what we used to have in bygone days; that was real weather for you and we'll never see its like again.

This is not hard to believe with the day that's in it today, but people have no cause for complaint yet until they inspect the potatoes. Then is the time they will start to worry, when they see them changing colour.

The story of the potato is well known hereabouts and what happened when it failed in years gone by, but may God grant it will not happen again!* Fear, though, haunts the sinner; it is his nature I suppose. It is man's way to struggle always to overcome fate, if only that were in his power. The human being is a strange animal, you agree, and stranger still is life, but what can we do about it, tell me that?

. . . A sad story the postman had for us this morning—the good

---

* Reference to the Great Famine. In the autumn of 1845 a blight struck the potato crop, on which the mass of the people were virtually dependent. Most of it was lost. In 1846 after a wet spring and humid summer the crop was a total failure.

33

and the bad are with us always. A man in the village was found dead in his bed after the night, God save us from the like of it! There is the human being with all his mad antics, say you, and look how death creeps up without warning, and neither stop nor stay possible. Death prevails over all the great powers of the world and I would say that only for him the world would have gone to the devil. As a Dunquin man put it, Death is the only gallant man left around these parts now, for nobody can get the better of that gentleman.

It is a man well on in years that lies dead today. Early in life he went to the States. He had neither wife nor family but, even if he hadn't, he had money to fall back on. Signs on it, some of the boyos will make a merry night of it tonight at the wake, for he was a good age, with no one crying after him. And, according to the order of things here these days, it is like a second wedding for the likes of him—goodbye to your life in this world and the blessing of God in the next!

I dare say it is no lament Micil will have tonight; instead he'll be singing 'An Spailpín Fánach' ('The Itinerant Labourer'), that's if they let him. The man gone is a grand-uncle of his nearing the four score years. May God be good to him and to all the dead who have gone on the way of truth!

I was conversing with Tom last night. He was grousing away like the devil because the visitors had all gone and there was no more free porter.

'Never mind that, Tom, there will come another day,' said I.

'There will,' he replied, 'but who will be spared to see it?'

'You'll last until next year on what you got soft from the visitors and they saved you enough money over the past quarter to keep you in drink well beyond Christmas, and haven't you them back again in no time at all.'

''Tis easy for you to talk, upon my soul, and it isn't your first time either. That's only a case of "Live, horse, and you will get grass". It would suit me better to have them here while I'm around myself than to be casting my lines and I getting no nibble at all.'

'That's life, Tom, every man with his own trouble, take it or leave it.'

. . . The rain is bouncing off the ground and, I promise you, the man that's out under it knows about it; it will drown the fleas on his back for him. Howsoever, as the old saying goes, 'It is bad to be caught in a gale, but sunshine follows the rain.'

There is no scrap of fish to be seen here for the past three weeks. There could not be, with the sea churned up every day and the rain pelting down on your poll from morning to night; things were never so bad.

There is great talk here about the two men from Canada who are proposing to imitate St Brendan and voyage across the high seas in their little coracle.* Most people here, I mean those who know anything about currachs, pay little heed to this wild talk. To be sure, the man who has lost his senses entirely may choose to bring that class of hardship on himself, for mad folk do the queerest things. Indeed, if they were to succeed in making the voyage it would be a miracle out and out. If the currach they have is anything like mine they will never make it. But, as they say here, it is always the same with moneyed people—they have more than they know what to do with.

And as for newspapermen, it is always the latest wonder with them. Take the meteor that fell from the sky not long since and how they had the poor creatures here frightened to death over it. But, on my soul, a lot of people have been shedding the ass's

* According to tradition, the sixth-century missionary, St Brendan, sailed from Brandon Creek, in his native Co. Kerry, to America in a boat made of leather. Tim Severin and his crew, in a boat built in similar fashion, made this journey in 1976–7. See Tim Severin, *The Brendan Voyage* (London, 1978).

skin for a good while now and it won't take long before it has dropped off all of them. They are growing tired of listening to far-fetched tales and you can't easily pull the wool over their eyes any more. Most of the simple folk around here died off years ago.

... The fuchsia took a battering last night; it has a colour as black as coal now and those lovely red bells that were on it have vanished for another year, whoever is spared to see them. The bite is in the wind always and it comes as no good sign. Corn and stacks are all in a tangle together and the spring sowing is in a sorry state. People say—not that they talk sense always—that when the farmer is riding high it goes to his head. Where now is all the great swaggering they had a little while back, defying the laws of the land and blocking the roads to prevent poor creatures from travelling to earn their hire.* Their case was different half a century or so ago; it was easy to catch them by the tail then!

... The two of us are here on our own today. It is ever said that strife is better than loneliness. No one minds seeing the back of mischief-makers and chatterboxes without sense. 'The sooner they leave, the better for us,' as the man said. Others would spend a while in your company, people who make good sense and who would not be trying to talk you down, and you would be sorry to see them go.

I don't know when the fine day will come. We keep hoping for a good month still. We have a wonderful Indian summer some years, especially if it rains on St Swithin's Day. 'There is hope of escape from prison but none from the grave.' Anyone that is alive will see a fine day some time. Many would argue

---

* Agitation against the Government over the price of milk.

that a man should give great thanks to God that he has a body to place in the grave.

The schools are open again and no great hurry on the children to attend. The human being is always rushing to turn his back on whatever is for his good, and plunging headlong into misfortune instead. He could be classed as an animal I suppose if he had no proper rearing—the most pitiful creature in existence I would say myself.

. . . I was conversing with Micil today and he related all that had happened on the night of the wake. There were two big barrels of porter at the wake-house, bread and tea, butter and jam galore, whiskey, fags and tobacco, lashings and leavings of everything. It was a wake night the likes of which has never been seen in the barony. And why not? Didn't himself leave orders that no man, woman, youngster, or child should go short on the night he was laid out; it would delight him to be watching them eating and drinking their fill, while he lay there stretched out dead and cold himself.

All was going fine but 'The devil take it,' says Micil, 'didn't I have to strike up 'An Spailpín Fánach' and 'twas how I ruined the rest of the night.'

'I fancy,' says I, 'you forgot entirely that the poor man was laid out there at all.'

'I did, wisha, and what's more, there was no thought in my head that anybody belonging to me was dead. What happened to myself was fine but, on my soul, some of the company there started going for each other's throats—ancient grudges and grievances left over from the past causing the ructions. Faith, I was shown the door myself and came home. How I managed it I don't rightly know for, on my soul and oath to you, my senses were scattered and they weren't hard to scatter since 'tisn't many of them I have.'

'That's how it goes, Micil, "an old woman's haul being pissed against the wall".'

'Yerra, man, isn't it the selfsame thing will cause all the hullabaloo when the parish priest hears about the ructions; won't he have a seven years' sermon over it?'

'Never mind that. What will he gain by it, only to be spouting away and wasting his breath? If the likes happens again, isn't it the same carry-on ye'll have? I suppose many a day and night will pass before there is such a wake again and some of us feel great need of the likes once a week at the least.'

The funeral is over, the corpse is under the clay and grass growing over him from now on. There were many mourners present and I never saw so many motor-cars at a funeral before, the second funeral here inside a week. The first was of a girl whose health has always been poor and it is a godsend to her to be lying under the ground free from pain and suffering, so long as there was no improvement in store for her. It is up to ten months since the last person was buried here and people say that it is many a long year since we had such a gap between funerals; now, once the graveyard gate has been opened, the corpses will be following each other for a good while to come. That's the way of the world. 'The rule of the churchyard is to let everyone in, the rule of the graveyard is to let no one out.'

. . . Well, there's a man going the rounds today, collecting money for the parish priest to keep the Seminary in Killarney going. The people here can't understand why all the collections are needed, more especially for this same Seminary. They argue that only the sons of bigwigs go there, people with money at the back of them, so there is no need for collections from the poor to educate them. But it's a waste of time talking. The rule of the headmen must be obeyed, though I don't know whether that will last for ever. The trouble with constant grumbling is

38

that there are those I fear who will use the affair for political ends.

Such is the talk amongst the 'simple' folk here and the people of today are not slow to do an about face.

There are heavy showers of rain pouring straight down out of the heavens, for there is not a puff of wind and there is hail mixed with the rain. I strolled back to the Square a while ago. One of the Civic Guard comes there to sign people on for the dole and the entire neighbourhood gathers, each man with his own slip of paper. Small farmers come with all their sons, each with his own slip of white paper too. They are highly satisfied with the life they have of it and you would hear some of them declaring that life in the Gaeltacht* has never been a patch on this. Their only fear is that it will not last. As Séamas Mháire put it, 'It won't last for ye'll ruin it yeerselves. The devil keeps busy.'

... The swell is washing up over the grass today and red seaweed floating at high tide, a man's depth of it in the water. No use is made of it these years, but there was a time when people would not have a wink of sleep for a week while they gathered it for winter manuring at this time of the year. They learned that it was too much trouble for little gain; the pack of guano was handier and it gives a better yield. 'Hard work teaches hard sense,' as the old saying goes.

I took a stroll for myself last night to the public house, my regular habit. I'm fond of the pint a couple of hours before I fling myself into the bed. I thought there wouldn't be a Christian in the wide world there before me and I would have my couple of hours enjoying myself there at my ease. But no

* Gaelic-speaking districts.

one should take his hopes for granted. The place was packed; men and women there, with no end of music, drink, and dancing, along with songs old and new.

If the people living around these parts in years gone by saw what goes on in public houses today they would make off up the hill or west across the bay rather than be looking at the way some folk have gone clean out of their senses, for that is how they would describe it. Isn't it the sad thing that they are gone from us, poor creatures that were never able to wet their lips with a drop.

. . . The Captain's lobster pots were driven ashore last night by high seas the like of which never came before. The fishing boats have been hauled up to the top of the slipway and there will be rot on them, I fancy, before they are moved again. The sea and the weather have gone to the devil entirely; nobody can fathom it. This was the season always when the fisherman made his living for the year, catching mackerel by night and shooting trawl-lines by day, with no stop from night till morning and from morning till night. A great help it was to make a living and in a good season a man had money to spare. It is strange what has befallen fishermen along this coast and it is patiently they are bearing it—they don't go knocking on the door of the Parliament or stretching themselves across the roads over it.* Nor will you find any picture of men like them in any of the country's newspapers. They take it all coolly and calmly and they are the very men who can. Furthermore, there are few fishermen left now, for most of those with any drive in them are over in the States or elsewhere overseas.

. . . A grand, glorious day. Everyone with a spark of youth left

* Reference to farmers protesting over the price of milk.

in him wants to be up and doing. The sun is shining brightly and the sky high and blue, except that there are a lot of white 'wethers' here and there, something I don't care for.

The saying has been passed down to us that 'the white fleece means rain', and the men of old knew what they were talking about.

Well, as I said before, there has to be talk and chatter, as long as a person has breath in him. If we stop 'tis a strange life we'll have of it and, without a doubt, if we continue talking non-stop the span allotted for talking will be over soon enough, even if we keep on heating our backsides at the fire.

Nuns I have with me here in the house for the past couple of hours and, wherever their like are, God's Paradise isn't the better for it. They come queening it for all the world as if they had been fruitful women, though that is not how they see themselves, but that they are humble creatures. They imagine nobody has the devil of a stroke to do, only sit down and spend the day swopping banter with them. The asses of Móinteán wouldn't stand it!

They have the Blasket books with them, asking about difficult words, if difficult they could be called. They tell me they are attending the University and have to study *An tOileánach* (*The Islandman*). They wanted me to explain the difficult words for them and I gave a fine, soft, smooth answer, saying I was no man of learning or training myself. Maybe, too, the men of learning might not accept my explanations.

Another thing I let fly at them was that the high-up learned professors and people with a sound knowledge of Irish were well paid to tease out the knotty problems for them; it was all a cod to be coming to myself for answers, while others were paid to give them. 'But,' says I, 'when I am paid in the same way as the professors are paid on yeer behalf, there will be no shortage of explanations for ye.'

'You are very hard on us,' says one of the nuns.

'If I am,' says I, 'I am not codding anybody. Faith, learning is not easily come by. Everyone giving ye an education is paid for it and ye receive payment for every pupil ye teach. But, no need to pay the simpletons a brass farthing! Let ye know from now on that the asses' ears are gone from the Gaelic-speakers of the Gaeltacht.'

'We thought you were a grand, calm, easy-going man, Seán,' one of the nuns tossed back at me, 'but we have a different opinion now.'

'"Examine the river well ere you trust yourself to the current," my good woman.'

Off out the door they trooped, the legs that brought them in stamping their disgust. If their prayers do any good, I don't suppose many of them will be offered up for my benefit!

Furthermore, people like these bring another thought to mind. They like to come to the Gaeltacht and meet the native speakers. Nuns, brothers, and priests are people that don't mix with anybody unless there is a Gaelic college there.* They gain little benefit from the same college which follows its own programme and rules. If they had somewhere where they could be persuaded to bring in native speakers for about three or four hours a day, you would see the difference this would make.

I have, with my own eyes, seen teachers of Irish that do more harm to the learner than good. How could it be otherwise when they cannot put two sentences together rightly or accurately? Not that I'm laying the entire blame on the heads of the teachers; they have made a wonderful effort but it is not to the Gaeltacht they should be sent as teachers of the language. You must have Gaelic from the cradle to be able to teach it properly—I yield to nobody in the world on that score. I am

---

* Summer schools for learning Irish.

only telling the gospel truth and truth never hanged anybody yet, though it can be bitter, they say.

... There were fishermen out trying for mackerel last night, the odd stray fish, but it is good to have the odd stray fish from time to time. That is the way with mackerel at this season of the year. If we had two months of settled, still weather with the sea calm and smooth men would have a regular livelihood, with fishing added to what they make on land. Calm means fish and a living; without calm you will have no fish.

Mackerel fishing was strong in this district at one period. Nobody is depending on it now for a living and devil the better he would be for it if he did. It was a wretched way of life for little gain and it is vanished and gone ever since the buyers gave up the curing. Fishing for mackerel went into decline and what is left now is only a shadow of what it was in the old days.*

... This is a great day of toil and sweat for the farmers. Their tongues are hanging out with the dint of work. They are saving and stacking corn that was flattened badly by the terrible gales we had during the past week. Believe me it is no Rose of Tralee Festival† that's bothering their heads but to have their sheaves stacked properly, and who can blame them? Today does not look too promising, only giving every sign that another bad bout is on its way. It seems as uncertain as a baby's bottom but we are due for a fine spell some time.‡

... There's a man in here with me now after travelling the

---

* In 1921 import duty of two dollars was imposed on each barrel of cured fish entering the USA. The market for cured fish disappeared.
† Beauty contest and festival held annually in Tralee in August.
‡ cf. 'Mr Dedalus, peering through his glasses towards the veiled sun, hurled a mute curse against the sky. "It's as uncertain as a child's bottom," he said.' (James Joyce, *Ulysses* (London, 1937), 3.)

whole country, he says, to find himself an ass. He has made the Dog with Eight Legs out of it for a story—where he went, who was talking to him, what he saw and how many pints of porter he drank during the two days of his search. Yesterday it was Baile Dháth, Feothanach, Ballybrack, and Ballinloghig; all the morning he has been across this southern side and with nothing to show for his trouble yet. He intends making neither stop nor stay until he travels west as far as Coum Strand. Money is no object, for he declares he will pay any price for a good ass.

'Whatever has happened to the asses,' I ask him, 'to say they're so scarce?'

'I'll tell you,' says he, 'there are two horse-dealers going round this barony at present and the ass hasn't the foal three weeks when they have paid out five or six pounds for it, and they getting a king's ransom in some other quarter for the same foal. So 'tis how, my dear man, that Maidhc has a job on to find an ass. However, I heard that Dónall back here has an old ass for sale, and as soon as I have this drop of tea swallowed, I'll head in his direction.'

'Dónall has the asses,' I said, 'but, if so, I fancy they're like O'Dunleavy's *Ass of the Fur* long ago:

> Stick a barrel of powder under his rump,
> Still you'll not make him budge or jump.*

Howsoever, follow your nose, Maidhc.'

... Maidhc strolls in to me again after spending the entire day long looking for an ass. He left neither house nor hovel from Kilcool west that he didn't poke his head into, and from there on to Glenaglanna. He sat down and an almighty thirst on him,

* A humorous song by the Blasket poet Seán O'Dunleavy about an ass he bought from the parish clerk.

but he would take no drop of tea from the 'Queen' even if she killed him. Any few potatoes left over and a mouthful of something salty were what he wanted, with a mug of water to wash them down.

We were not long after finishing the dinner then and, as luck would have it, there was a fine lump of boiled salt eel's head left over along with a good few grand floury Champions, potatoes Maidhc is not very used to. They wouldn't grow for himself, he says, for it is soil for Banners he has, not that he cares in the devil so long as he sees some sort of potato.

He cleared all that was placed in front of him, to the very bone of the eel's head which had disappeared. He made short work of the lot and he needed no coaxing. He made the sign of the Cross over himself and thanked us. He hauled out his pipe, stuffing it with black tobacco; in no time at all we had 'the Saturday boat' there in the kitchen and we not able to see one another for smoke.

When he seemed to be feeling at ease, with his belly full and enough of the pipe smoked, I began by asking him how he had fared since morning. By way of reply he began ranting and raving and I own to you, on my solemn oath, that if many of those that crossed his path are above ground tomorrow morning, it is the four-leafed shamrock they must possess! Even the Germans didn't escape a lashing nor the English, but it was the horse-dealers that he damned most of all. As long as I have been in this world I never heard curses the like of them in the mouth of any man.

'Go to this fellow and go to that fellow! But there isn't an inch of ground that I haven't travelled from here west, and only no for an answer.'

'Whisper,' says I, 'did you call at Dónall's? He had asses for sale always.'

'Upon my soul I did, wisha, and 'twas he gave me the neat,

smart answer. He had a mare ass, you see, so I asked him a very simple question, why had she no foal. Well, if you heard the answer that fellow gave me: he had a mare he much preferred to her and she had no foals!'

Dónall is a man whose wife is without child, but Maidhc of the Ass was unaware of this.

'They have the ready tongue westwards of us too, Maidhc, upon my soul.'

'That's nothing, wisha, compared to what you would hear when you go among the Móinteán and Muileann people. They're the boyos with the ready tongue for you.'

'Lamb of God, whatever has happened to the same Móinteán, a place where there were always thousands of asses, Maidhc?'

'Amn't I after telling you that the foal is hardly born there now before somebody is on the spot wanting it, and tossing over whatever sum you care to name; the price is no object, he must have the foal.'

'It will be hard for you to find an ass, Maidhc.'

He is a widower and holding his head higher nowadays than ever before, so says I:

'It is easier to find a woman than an ass these times.'

'I dare say any one of them would do to keep us warm at this day of our life, but whatever about the ass, may God and his Blessed Mother preserve us from the women! We saw enough of them.'

. . . I strolled out this morning, if morning you could call it. Ten o'clock had struck and it was time for any tinker to be hitting the road. I called in for a while to see a next-door neighbour as is my normal habit. He would think it a strange morning that I paid him no visit. He is 86 years of age and he has all his wits and senses still.

It is a strange world to him today with the mad rush there is on everybody, and they having everything under the sun within their reach. If some of those that are growing grass were living now, they would say people have heaven on earth today.

'There's no use talking,' says I to him, 'this is the modern way of life and, if peace lasts and no war breaks out, 'tis only better it will be getting for us, if God spares us to see it. Did you hear,' I went on, 'that men landed on the moon last night?'

'I did not hear, wisha, and even if I did 'tis little heed I would pay to it. And I swear upon my own soul that I cannot give in to you either, even though you're not one for telling lies. That's a place where no one will ever go and they shouldn't be thinking of it either.'

'Give over now. A goodly part of your life is gone and isn't it many the thing you've seen that you never expected to see at all. You would not have believed that a car would be travelling the roads without horse or ass drawing it until you had to skip fast out of its way or be left stone-cold dead. Sure, that's no great number of years ago and look at the craft flying up in the sky since then. That's something else you would never have believed at one time in your life, so isn't it as well for you to accept that men have gone to the moon now?'

'Whatever I shall or shall not see, the moon is different from any other place. What people used to say long ago was that the moon is a great ball of fire and anything going within two hundred miles of it would be burnt to ashes.'

'Isn't there many a thing we used to be told like that, Micí, and there wasn't a word of truth in it, but after last night you have a different story about the moon.'

''Tis no use you telling me that men have gone to the moon, for I simply will not believe it from you and there's no sense in it for a tale.'

Even if I kissed his arse he would not credit it at all, so I took my leave and faced west for the forge. There were enough horses there to make war on the Crown and you would say to yourself that the poor blacksmith had a heavy day's work in front of him. Seán Fada was there holding forth with the same old blather out of him as always. The big wind that blew in the middle of the week he was going on about and, whatever force was in the wind, Seán made it five times worse. I said, to provoke him, that it had been nothing like as fierce as he was making out.

'Listen, will you, to the man from the Island,' said Seán, 'trying to make out I don't know what I'm talking about!'

'We're all right,' I retorted, 'so long as we only listen while the people of Márthan fire shit at us!'

According to him a gust of wind had swept away a stack of corn from its moorings in his haggard and dropped it in the river a hundred yards away, right way up, without so much as a sheaf falling out of it.

'Good boy you are,' says I, 'be blathering away to them, for that is how you were reared.'

'The curse of God on you and your likes,' says he, ''tis a waste of time talking to you!'

'You didn't hear the latest news that's after coming out?' I said to him now.

'Upon my soul, I did not. 'Tis little news I'll hear from anyone excepting yourself only.'

'I like my job, faith, to be gathering news and telling it to you while the fellows you stand drinks to would never tell you a thing.'

'Sure, that's the way of the world. "The helping hand is the hand faulted." And maybe if I kept the grip of the drowning man on my money, people would be more ready to tell me their news. Never mind about me being too soft, my lad, but tell me what you have heard.'

'Well, on my soul, any old pensioner that's living on his own and has someone coming in to see to him, or doing anything for him, that person will be getting an allowance too now for looking after him.'

''Tis hard for me to give you the lie, and though I believe everything you say, devil sense or reason is there to it for a tale.'

'Oh, there is surely, when you understand it properly and it's explained in detail to you. If you're sick or laid up at home tomorrow, who is going to lift the latch on your door? Who will give you bite or sup and who is going to do any hand's turn for you? And if there isn't anyone, won't you have to be taken to the hospital, where somebody will have to look after you? And that will not be done without money. Everyone working there is well paid, and they with enough on their hands already without you being placed as an extra burden on top of them. And there's something else, the hospital will take your pension so you will be paying for yourself more or less while you are there. And wouldn't it be a comfort to you to have your son or your daughter or some relation calling in and attending to you in your own little house?'

'There's sense to that for a story now and 'tis welcome to my ears, but I'm only afraid it can't be true; that it's too good to be true.'

'It is not too good at all. The old-age pensioners are not with us long and what does it matter so long as they are given help and fair play at the latter end of their days? Haven't they done their share? Anyone that reaches the pension age, isn't it many the day's work he has done for the country? You never heard, seemingly, that Cáit here above is drawing it for calling in to see her father now and again.'

'God knows I would believe that, for if anyone in the world is drawing the allowance, she will be the first woman in Ireland to get her hands on it; there is nothing in the kid's belly or the goat's udder but she knows about it. Do you know how much a person would draw for looking after a poor pensioner or someone in my case?'

'Going by what I heard, a person can pick up ten shillings a day for looking after someone and that is what Cáit is getting for looking after her father.'

'Lamb of God, sure isn't that more than the pensioner himself gets?'

'That's the law that's laid down. You have three pounds a week pension now when all you have to do is pull on your trousers, so is it how you imagine that somebody else would be cleaning up after you and getting your meals ready free, gratis, and for nothing? That's not how things are at all, but ye pensioners are to be kept clean and comfortable at the latter end of yeer days.'

''Tis as well for me so to go and tell Mary to put in for it directly. You haven't your fish until you've landed him, and may God spare you life and health for opening my eyes for me.'

'But all the money in the world is little good to you. The health is the jewel and blessing for the sinner because when that turns against you, what use is money to you? "The health before the wealth".'

. . . Micí rambles in to me fairly early in the morning to ask the latest news. I fire away with whatever comes into my head, and it is all equal to him whether it's the truth or the most unlikely tale ever, so long as the frame of truth is put on it.

He put many questions to me about the public house, for he is a man that has an almighty fondness himself for the drop.

'We had a great night of it last night, with strangers and Yanks there; 'twas only a case of "Drink your fill, Micheál." I never saw a night there to beat it yet.'

'I suppose the artful lads were hovering round them?'

'Oh, 'pon my soul they were, and they didn't stay fishing off one point only, but were taking careful soundings always; if they were getting no nibble on the hook they would soon be hauling in; with their glass in their fist they would have changed to some other corner.'

'That is something I would believe, for those artful lads never failed yet. Lamb of God! What a great life it is for drink, or where do people find the money for it at all? I'm convinced the country must be overflowing with it.'

'Yerra, man, what makes you say that? Haven't they money now and they leaving the mother's womb? Isn't the mother drawing money as soon as she starts carrying the child, and after the child is born hasn't she her full purse of it to collect? It isn't the same as in your day at all.'

'God and Mary his Mother pity my day! That was a poor and wretched time, when our only enemy was another child to be on its way and not a scrap there for those we had already. If the people that went through that life were here now and saw the life today they would have their knees worn out from praying. And look at them today. 'Tis how most of them never say a prayer at all. God help us, but isn't it the strange world!

'Have we long more to wait for Friday?'

'Not long. The day after tomorrow.'

''Tis the long week. It seems like two months since it was here last. If I am spared, I'll knock sparks out of the night, for however good the life we lead, we'll have to leave it behind us.'

'Upon my soul that was a great night's porter Tom Dubh had of it last night and by the same token isn't he every day as old as yourself, so why must you be waiting till Friday before tossing a sup of it back? If I were in your boots it is not by day I would go north at all but by night. There's nobody about during the day, sure. Isn't it at night the goat is put roasting in public houses; and here's another thing—isn't it many the drop would come your way soft without costing you a halfpenny? When will you ever catch Tom Dubh drawing his pension in a morning as you do, or in the middle of the day for that matter? Isn't it fine and sensible he is for himself? He could teach more of ye.'

'Oh, by my palms, boy, there is no woman keeping her eye on Tom, and there never was, but whatever way he is dragging along I do not begrudge him and never did. Tom has often said that he knows men that never touch a drop but would drink themselves to death if they came by it soft. I'm not so sure if it isn't the same case with Tom himself.'

There was an edge to his tongue and I had a notion he was rather envious of Tom. He had his two eyes fixed on me and you would wonder whether he was giving in to me at all or not; I believe he wasn't and that he suspected I was making it all up.

'I don't know,' I said, making light of it all as my last word, for he would stay gabbing there till next morning, 'I don't know whether 'tis better to piss it away or shit it away in the heel of the hunt.'

''Pon my soul,' he replied, 'whatever we'll do with it, Tom is letting it fly both ways.'

'Good day to you,' I said. He left me with every guffaw out of him.

. . . Many horses in the forge today and the farmers moaning and groaning over the weather. The blacksmith is telling them that it is not bad enough for himself at all, for if it was fine nobody would come near him. But it is proper forge weather, wet, dirty, misty, and no knowing where the sun has gone.

Bod and Com were out fishing last night, with only the two of them in the currach. People said they must be on their way to Newfoundland. Part of the night was spent waiting for them to come home to see if they would have the fish to grill on the tongs, but morning had brightened before they landed back. A huge sea-animal had got himself tangled in the nets and they spent the night dragging him after them so as not to lose their nets. He was thirty feet long with a body to match and he weighing about three hundred-weight.* They would have had a decent catch of mackerel if he had not fouled their nets at the first cast, for they had a hundred fine mackerel in the nets besides him. If the weather settled there would be fish along the coast; it is the time for it.

. . . Father Pádraig calls in to see me and a man from the Island along with him. The 'Queen' of the house was not at home, so off they went to Ballinloghig where they found her. It was evening by this time with the night drawing in. He said that after he had swallowed a bite it would be time to face for Bóthar where they were going to have a night of it. Many strangers would be there and a good drop in the teats† by some of them, with the boyos to milk them only raring to go.

. . . The 'Doctor' is home on holiday from England. You would swear on your solemn oath that he had never spent a day away from home, his Gaelic accent is so good. He is a great man for the drink and, that being so, a lot of the hounds are on the look-out for him. They drop anchor in no public house until he comes in. It will be lowered close alongside him then and I promise you it will stay below until closing time.

He brought an Englishman home with him but two nights were all he lasted before the udder ran dry. I would say it is udder trouble that will bring the 'Doctor's' own gallop to a halt.

* A species of whale, most likely; cf. *The Islandman*, chap. 23, and *Twenty Years A-Growing*, chap. ix.
† Money to stand drinks.

It is the likes of the 'Doctor' would suit the artful lads of this place. But, as a rule, their own cow will not be giving milk, never fear, for you will find one of these fellows there from ebb to high tide and, unless they're caught napping, they never dip their hands in their own pockets. The artful lads are there always and always will be. But as the old woman from Ballybooley said, if everyone was a bishop, there would be no priests.

. . . I was talking with Bod a while ago and he told me he would try for mackerel again tonight. The weather has turned much milder but we have a half moon and this does not suit the mackerel too well; though if it is travelling in shoals as is usual with it at this time of the year, moon or sun won't scatter it. We have had bad weather for some time now and that is what breaks up and scatters the shoals.

. . . A couple of men call in to me in the afternoon after coming from Dublin. Two hefty fellows they were and a match for each other in height and girth, a fine healthy cut to them and they showing all the signs of good feeding. They had a motor car and were, I fancied, out for a high time of it. They wanted a place to stay for a couple of nights and this was found, good stabling that suited them.

I took to them at once for they were clearly two open-handed, generous fellows. They spoke Gaelic exactly as I speak it myself. They were chatting and gabbing away and peppering me with searching questions about this corner of the country. Had we music and dancing and drink here and, above all else, were there plenty of women about?

Well, says I in my own mind, beyond all that ever crossed my path so far, the pair of ye are out for the devil's own high jinks.

Midday

They set up their last and their awls in their lodging house and, in no time at all, they had the kettle boiled and a grand pot of tea made for themselves. It is many the woman would not lay the table as neatly as Séamas did. Séamas and Paddy their names were. I took my leave of them but, as I was going, Paddy asked me to make sure to spend the night in their company; they needed a guide and I was their man if I were game for it.

'Upon my soul,' says I to them, "tis God sent ye to me.'

Eight o'clock came and off we went west, as far west as we could go. When we came to Brú na Gráige* Séamas said it was many the day he had spent there. I pricked up my ears at this and told myself that Séamas was no greenhorn; he had served his apprenticeship in full with the people of Clochar and Dunquin.

'Seánín de hÓra† is alive yet, I suppose?'

'Alive and kicking,' I told him.

'I must call in to see him tomorrow, wisha, and get him to tune up.'

We arrived at Dunquin and had a drink there. In no time at all the public house was filling up. A fine strapping girl walks in the door, and the skirt only reaching half-way down her thighs. Paddy nudged Séamas and Séamas nudged me.

The musicians arrived and soon the sets were being danced and my two boyos, skilled dancers, out there in the thick of it. Each of them had found a partner, Séamas dancing with the girl with the bare thighs, and if he wasn't pounding the floor from one end of the house to the other! More sets were danced and more drinks downed.

'She's the grand mare,' said Paddy to Séamas.

'I never expected to find anyone like her here.'

---

* Hostel for boys learning Gaelic.
† Well-known local singer and musician.

55

'Anyone like her here!' said I. ''Tisn't any shortage of women will be your trouble here, boy.'

Until Séamas heard me saying that, he imagined I was the kind of man who would not like to see the lamb straying from the ewe.

There was no holding them now and, by the way they were going, I thought it was dead they would be carried home. But there is no limit to men who know their trade. When closing time was called they came over to me like two priests.

Five nights they spent gallivanting like that, but I spent only two nights in their company for they had special invitations to the houses where these fine women were staying. But the day came in the end when they had to take their leave. I was not sorry, even though I was lonesome after them, but they had me driven clean out of my senses. I could not keep pace with them for these were men in their prime.

. . . I strolled out last night to be among the company, my usual custom. The 'Queen' in the corner here tells me that I won't give up until the knees buckle under me; I'll have to stop then and serve me right! I let her words fly past me as the swan lets the water, for if I made her any answer she would have the better of me.

I walked in the door of the public house to join the company. I gazed about; a man was singing and I could swear by the book and the English Bible that I knew him well. There was not a whisper to be heard while the song lasted—signs of a good singer always, when he is given hush and quiet in a house, especially a public house. This my man had with the best of good manners.

After a while he comes over and a fine big pint glass of porter in his hand for me. He stretches out his hand saying, 'How are you at all, Seán of the Island?'

'Unless I'm mistaken, 'tis Lar Phidí I have,' I said.

'The same, wisha.'

'You were only a schoolboy when I was a grown man in Dunquin.'

'It was a great guess by you after thirty years.'

We started reminiscing and putting one and twenty questions to each other; if we were there yet we would have had more questions. His people went to County Meath long years ago.* Of course people are not so cut off from one another as they used to be half a century ago. As the man told me last night, he has Dublin on the doorstep now. I had little notion in the morning that Lar Phidí of the County Meath would be there before me at the 'Well' in the evening.

... I was having a lie down on the old bed after a feed of Champion potatoes and a cured mackerel. My pipe was stuffed with dear tobacco and a cloud of smoke was floating out through the top of the window when I heard the man's voice outside:

'Is there anyone alive in this house?'

'There is, by my baptism,' I called up from the bed; his was a voice I knew well. I rose up and who had come in to stand on the hearthstone but my friend Liam Browne from Ballybunion.

'I have a motor car outside,' he said, 'so come along north with me.'

The car was there shining and off we drove north to the 'baptism well', as Liam called it. The teachers in Listowel had special holidays at this time because the race meeting was on,† so they decided to spend a day in the Gaeltacht listening to the locals.

---

* Some people from the barren Gaeltacht areas along the western seaboard were resettled by the Irish Government on good farmland in the east of the country.
† The three-day Listowel Races held annually in September.

Liam was their leader and guide. The blessed balm was freely bestowed upon us and we had music and songs to our hearts' content. There was dancing too, Irish and every other kind they fancied and, before the end of the day, the squabbling dance flared up amongst them and we were shown the door then, all of us together. Maybe it was for the best. Nothing lasts long. The squabbling itself does not last.

... There are visitors about still, lads and lasses from Cork University. They are not without knowledge of Gaelic, no more than they are of anything else. They drink a drop, male and female students alike, and they swallow any drink, from the bottles on the top shelf to the barrel of porter on the floor. Some of the lads sport beards or long whiskers on their chins while others are as clean-shaven as the bishop. As for the girls, some are well covered up, while others are showing a lot of thigh. They give every example under the sun to the local people. Some of them would let you suck free porter from the teat* while two or three would go on the teat themselves if it was available, which it seldom is here.

If you have Gaelic let it fly at them, that is what they want. But, so far as the local lads are concerned, it is little reward they get for their Gaelic from the girls because, as soon as night falls each of them has her own escort.

... I called in to see Murchadh recently. I asked him if there was any news in the morning paper.

'The dickens a thing, wisha, but do you see the two mackerel I have there grilling on the tongs, the two fattest mackerel I have seen for years? I had them barely laid across the tongs when they caught fire on me. I won't be able to grill them this

---

* They would stand the locals drinks.

night and I with the longing of the drowning man for them, not to mind being starved with the hunger.'

I told him to raise the tongs well up above the fire and they would grill fine in their own oil. Before long they were cooking nicely. The savoury smell coming from them would raise the dead from their graves. He lifted them on to a plate in the middle of the table and it did not take him long to make a clean sweep of them. A mad longing for the fish came over myself. 'A child covets whatever he sees.' But, upon my soul, he did right to eat them himself. Only a stepmother would blame him for it. He left the bones for the cat.

When he finished the meal he turned to me saying, 'Hunger is the best sauce of all, and then to have something tasty to eat. I have nearly burst my navel with them.' He was wanting to chat now and you have to listen to Murchadh.

'Have you any thought of marrying?' I ask him. He is a man that steered clear of marriage always.

'Marry is it? The man that marries is out of his mind. Look at that tomcat of mine there; he's a great example to myself. Whenever he feels the urge, out he goes and he doesn't come back until he has seen to his needs. That's the life I want too.'

'But isn't there the life to come, Murchadh, boy?'

'We have enough to do coping with this life, without bothering with the next.'

'Don't let the priest hear you, Murchadh, boy'.

'Don't bring up religion, priest or minister to me. I never saw one of them yet but he was living the life of a lord. The cat has the right religion.'

'Talking about marriage we were.'

'Yes, we were talking about marriage. Isn't it the convenient marriage the cat has, to be roving in and out.'

'But that is not what was intended for the human being, surely.'

'I have heard it said that 'tis pleasing to have the mistress of the house waiting for a man with everything laid out on the table. The table without her is more pleasing by far. Wouldn't it be the nice life I'd have, don't you think, to be coming home to a grousing devil of a wife? Peace has its price boy, ever and always.'

'But don't you ever feel lonesome at night?'

'Lonesome at night? Why ever should I be? Who is there to pry on you? And what prize would I be for any woman? Sure, amn't I the worst-looking picture in the world. Isn't it how anyone who came in and took one look at me would not be able to clear out the door fast enough.'

I left the matter there and took my leave, for I knew only too well that it was useless arguing with him. In any case all we wanted was the crack* for a while.

On the road eastwards I put my head in at the door of the forge. Five or six horses were waiting outside to be shod. The blacksmith was hopping mad inside—a fair and market day in Dingle and he not able to be there over 'the bastards of farmers'. He told them they must put a stop to it once and for all; not to come near him on a fair day ever again, or on a Saturday either.

'What the devil use is money to me if I am stuck in here from Monday to Saturday and from morning to night, without ever catching a glimpse of sun or wind from dawn to dusk, and I only like a snail would be in its shell?'

Nobody made him an answer, for he's the class of a man that would knock you down flat in the heat of the moment and give you his heart's blood half an hour later. One of the farmers there had a big heavy horse that was acting rather fidgety for shoeing, so he decided he would return home until the

* Conversation, chat.

blacksmith had got over that fit of temper. He was just leading the horse away when the blacksmith saw him.

'Where do you think you're going, you son of a whore?' says he to the poor devil outside. 'I am sending nobody home today. Isn't the day wasted now and faith I'd be left with neither one thing nor the other.'

The horse needing four shoes was given only two so that the blacksmith could attend to them all before night fell. The sweat was pouring down his cheeks, a red fire was blazing up, with no word out of anybody except the blacksmith himself and he giving out without sparing his language. If the horse happened to stir, a belt of the hammer was what he got across the ribs. If ever any place resembled hell, it was the forge with the blacksmith and the horses and the glowing fire.

... There are divers here for some time diving in the Blasket Sound. There is a great pile of gold, they say, in an old vessel that went to the bottom long years ago, and they are trying to find it.

I remember and I a child when, leaving after a ramble to a neighbour's house, we would be told we would meet the old woman from Spain on the way home that night. I did not understand too well then who the old woman was, or how the story came about.

A lady was found drowned, it seems, on the Island Strand at the time when the *Santa Maria de la Rosa** foundered. According to old stories about her she was a wealthy woman; she wore many rings and bracelets of gold and was buried at Castle Point† where the graveyard is today. She was not

---

* A flagship of the Spanish Armada, wrecked off Dunmore Head in 1588.
† Castle of Piaras Ferriter, poet-chieftain of West Kerry (*c.*1600–53).

buried, strange to say, in the graveyard proper but outside it. Years ago an old man showed me the spot.

If those divers fail to find the ship's gold in the Island Sound, it is very likely they will rob the grave if anyone points it out to them. Maybe the rings and bracelets are buried with the old woman. It is only a case of 'maybe' of course, but it is the same 'maybe' with the ship, I fancy.

... Donnchadh Bán has Diarmaid O'Shea working for him building a couple of rooms on to his house. Donnchadh wants Diarmaid to be giving him all his time, but Diarmaid only puts in a day now and again and Donnchadh is hopping mad with him. Donnchadh has placed the grant with Séamas Tom and has ordered the windows from him, but Séamas has brought no window yet that fits. This is Diarmaid's excuse. Donnchadh is obliged to listen, for Diarmaid has taken the wind out of his sails.

Donnchadh's wife pokes her head into the affair, and dumb she certainly is not.

'Blast you!' she lets fly at Diarmaid, 'that didn't come with a week and all in the house driven to distraction by you. You're no better than a tinker, 'tis long ago the work would have been finished by Muiris Sheáinín, but you think you're sitting pretty.'

Diarmaid listens to her with the calm of the dead, for it is well he knows the ways of tradesmen. What Donnchadh's wife does not know is that a tradesman will not come poaching in another's preserve without his leave.

'Whisper,' says Diarmaid to her, 'where are the windows?'

'My curse and the curse of God down on Séamas Tom's poll!' says she. 'I'm all at sixes and sevens for the past half-year with him, coming here and nothing ever right by him.'

'You'll have to take the grant off him. Didn't I advise you the first day ever not to let him have it?'

She turns on her husband next. 'Stir yourself, Donnchadh, and jump on your bicycle. Tell him to have the windows here in the morning; that Diarmaid will be waiting for them.'

'The devil I will, wisha,' says Donnchadh.

The upshot of it all was that she rode off herself, for it is a woman's bicycle they share between them. Howsoever, she came back with no great satisfaction, for there was nobody at home in Séamas Tom's place.

But what is killing her entirely today is that Séamas has come with the windows, but where is Diarmaid? Back in Dunquin, that's where, building another house and everything to hand by him according as he wants it.

'But,' Diarmaid said to me afterwards, 'I would prefer to have nothing to do with it. I would rather go to the Glen of the Mad* than come working here where nothing whatever is right. You have two masters over you, each of them giving different orders. I let them rant away but where's the peace? If I paid any heed to them wouldn't it be worse for me than the hardest day's work I ever did? "Peace is everything", boy.'

. . . I met Philib today and whenever I do I have sport. He is a grand, easy-going, innocent man and you can say what you like to him. He doesn't recognize the difference between truth and fancy, and I don't know that he cares so long as it whiles away part of the day. Isn't it all one to him, sure, and isn't it all one to us too if we had proper sense!

'A great job my son, Dónall, has got,' says he to me.

'A notable job, by my baptism.'

'It is, 'pon my soul. He is the man appointed now by the Department of Lands to be the gelder of stallions and young

---

* In West Kerry where, it is said, mad people lived wild, who were too swift to be caught.

sows from Slea Head eastwards and on north to Churl's Cove, and in as far as Dingle.'

'That's a great job, Philib, if only the stallions were plentiful. But what matter so long as he has a foot in the door of the Department. They know a good man when they see one.'

I don't know, says I to myself, whoever told him that for a yarn. The son himself, I suppose, for well able he is to tell them. I was moving on when he put a question to me about Maidhc Thomáisín's wife.

'Is it true that she had twins on top of all the children she has already?'

'I couldn't say,' I told him, 'but it is a story I would credit. In my opinion it's not difficult to set her on the way; some women are like that.'

. . . They are grumbling like the devil here for some while over the amount of money the priest is asking from them. They think it strange entirely that the priest's house is being knocked down and a new one costing a sackful of money is being built in its place. It was the chapel a couple of years ago with a mountain of money spent on it, but they had recovered from that, the wound was healed and the scab gone; that wound has been reopened now and red war is on.

Such is the hullabaloo about priests and presbyteries and money, so that folk are growing sick of the whole affair, not of course that everybody looks at things in the same light; there are those who simply don't bother their heads about it at all, but there are more who do.

What people complain most about these days is the sermons. They can't stand great long sermons, teachings according to Paul and Matthew, teachings that people for the most part pay no heed to excepting the odd poor simple soul in the congregation, and they are becoming a rare breed!

Midday

They have been putting up with that kind of blather for too long now. A short sermon on fresh topics would arouse interest, but interest flags if it is long drawn out. The shorter the sermon the sweeter it is, and well the priest knows this himself. They will come to their senses when it is too late, when they have no congregation left to listen to them and, you never know, but that time may be nearer than you think.

. . . There are red ructions in Baile Uí Sheáin today, the same as yesterday. The cause of it all was a son of Philib's that fired 'a shot' at Máire Mhór's daughter who lives west of us here. Máire's daughter has a young baby now and she not married yet. What a rumpus and ree-raa! The baby is a couple of months old, with Máire trying to get the father to own the child, small blame to her. There is blue murder going on.

Máire took the bus this morning, shepherding the daughter and baby, her husband and two of her sons on board. She made neither stop nor stay until she landed at Philib's house and the load with her. Philib was caught unawares with no notion at all that lightning would strike. Philib's wife was expecting the visitors but as little and wasn't in, as it happened, to receive the load. She was quickly on the scene, though, and went into battle.

'Jump on your horse,' says she to Philib, 'and fetch the Guards to the house to clear out this filth quick and smart.'

Off rode Philib, but faith Máire and her brood never budged. The Guards' barrack is not far from Philib's place and he was not gone long before he was back to report to his wife Bríde that the Guards take no hand or part in cases of 'stray shots' like that. Then Bríde started the battle all of a sudden. She made a grab for the young woman and her child to drive them out but Máire was only spoiling for the fight. No sooner had Bríde laid hands on the mother of the child than she had the shawl whipped off her own head and was twisting it round Bríde's neck. She would have choked her then and there only for her husband begging her, in God's name, not to have Bríde's death on her hands.

Máire loosened her grip at her husband's pleading and told Bríde that if she saw her lifting a finger again she would need the priest with the last sacraments by the time she had finished with her. But, on my soul, didn't Bríde flare up again. Máire was close enough, though, to spring headlong at Bríde a couple of times, leaving her to lick her wounds. Poor Philib was trying to quieten things down all the while and the poor son was full of shame and misery over the story. At last he found his voice.

'There's no cure for it, Dad, but to go and bring the proper man here and make a clean job of the affair. It would be better than all this uproar.'

'That's admitting it,' Máire Mhór cried. 'He's admitting it out of his own mouth.' And she was crowing over it.

'I suppose so,' said Philib, for all poor Philib wanted was peace, even if he had to buy it dear. 'I think it is the best way to settle it.'

But all the fire had not gone from Bríde yet.

'Clear off out of my fine house, ye scum of the parish, and don't be putting yeerselves on the same level as respectable folk. It is a long time, and a very long time . . .'

'Peace from God to us,' said poor Philib.

'Look,' said Máire at last when she sensed that the iron in the fire was getting soft, 'Look, it isn't dead anyone is. Wasn't it only heat of the blood was the cause of all, and if a young woman and her child move into any house, sure it couldn't happen unless God's blessing was on that house.'

The upshot of all the commotion was that the priest was sent for, and if the priest was not the proper judge of the case, who could be? There was no second word about it when Philib gave his son leave to go and marry the young woman for himself.

They made a great wedding-day of it in Buailtín,* the likes of which had not been seen since the Dingle Massacre.† Bríde and Philib came home in the evening bringing their new care with them, the little foal along with the mother. And, as the man said, it is often a man and his wife spent a long while hoping for such a child and it never came!

. . . Bod and Com went past a little while ago and they sitting in a motor car! A couple of local men these are, and they heading for Ballydavid to go out fishing. Nothing would do them but to travel through the village here in a motor like two important gentlemen. If they hadn't been given a lift in the car, it is along Bóthar na Léinsí they would have gone, the short cut down. But this was better, for people would be talking and there's nothing like setting tongues to wag awhile. The boot was crammed with their nets and oilskins, and the pair giving every shout out of them as they were being driven west.

Talking with Murchadh I was when they came by. The car stopped and Bod spoke:

'Would you mind, gentlemen, directing us on the right road for Ballydavid?'

'The devil sweep ye, wisha, ye pair of blackguards, it will be a long while surely before either of us needs to put ye on the right road for Ballydavid, so long as there's a "well"‡ there to draw ye!'

My impression was that the stranger driving the car did not

* i.e. Ballyferriter.
† On one occasion during the Land War in the nineteenth century thousands gathered in Dingle to demand reductions in rents from the landlords. Fourteen were killed and several wounded by British soldiers.
‡ Public house.

understand a word of what passed between them. He wouldn't have been any the wiser for it if he did. There was a smirk on Bod's face, so you would swear it was his blessing Murchadh had bestowed upon him.

'Thank you, gentlemen,' says Bod. He spoke with such care that you would think he was a learner of Irish.

'Do you know what? We have taken to this place!'

Visitors they were, forsooth, and they were gone before Murchadh could get his speech back to send a proper prayer flying after them. There was every guffaw out of the pair of them and they driving away.

'Isn't it fine for those two?' says I after the car had gone.

'Isn't it the story of the cat all over again? Ne'er a care in the world but to fill your belly with whatever you come across, good or bad; to while away the day, fall into bed for yourself and rise as you please. And if it happens that you don't wake up at all, there's nobody bothering their heads over you and what the devil do you care?'

'I don't know, wisha, Murchadh, but surely you would be better off having a little woman in the house than to be a lone bachelor traipsing the parish. Isn't a man without a wife like a vessel without a rudder?'

''Tis well you know it was no shortage of women that was my trouble; 'twas how they were in a mad scramble with one another after me once of a day, and a woman would bed with me still. I just never had enough courage. Where marriage is concerned 'twas the case with me always that it was a real tug of war between memory* and common sense, with neither of them ever getting the upper hand.'

'How well Bod and Com took a wife and care upon themselves, when all's said and done.'

* i.e. of the hardship of his parents struggling to feed their family.

'Isn't it there you have it again? Isn't it to a man with a head on his shoulders you would go looking for sense, and notice how these have it too despite all their gallivantings? If I wanted an ounce of sense tomorrow morning isn't it to one of that pair I would turn? The day would be a long time coming before either of them turned to me, and small blame to them.'

'I'm afraid, Murchadh boy, that you will have to give up the cat for your example.'

'I'm inclined to think 'tis a bit late in the day for me now,' said Murchadh.

I left him then and set off towards Ballydavid after the two scallywags. A currach was just leaving the slipway there when I arrived and my pair aboard, who else? They made no delay at the 'well', says I to myself. It was seldom with them not to be taking the big boat out but maybe the Captain wasn't prepared to venture out that night and they were left depending on the cockleshell.

The weather did not look too promising and I judged that the most they could do was make a run out, give one cast of the nets and head straight home. That is just what happened. I was mending a couple of lobster pots meanwhile. They had been battered about in the sea for the past fortnight and it was God's own luck that I found them at all.

I had just finished mending the pots when we managed to catch sight of the currach heading for the shore. It had been dark for some while with wind and showers from west and south.

The currach pulled in by the slip and they had six hundred mackerel after the trip. One cast of the nets was all they had made. The entire catch went to Dingle and it fetched three pounds per hundred. They didn't even take a single mackerel home to grill on the tongs, for they would have had to break into the hundred. This is something the fisherman does not do as a rule unless the weather were fine, with fish plentiful and it fetching no price. They wouldn't mind breaking into the hundred then and sharing the fish with poor creatures in need. So, it wasn't from any meanness that the entire haul went to Dingle.

As soon as the Captain saw the catch the other two buckos had made, he was all impatience to take the boat out himself, but didn't the pair of them refuse to crew for him. They were not best pleased, I dare say, over the refusal they had received themselves before that. Two *jaingléirí** the Captain found to go with him and, though they were out an hour and a half, they returned without a single fish. He was cursing like mad and it is the poor *jaingléirí* that were at the receiving end. The Captain is the very devil!

... Mártan and his wife Sinéad are all the sport in Baile Uí Sheáin today, and any day there will be entertainment in that village little of it escapes us here too.

Sinéad is as hot-tempered as Mártan is easy-going but they both suffer from the same complaint, if complaint it can be called. They live in dread of the evil eye and there isn't a charm in Ireland they don't know about and have not faith in. There are some people of course who only pretend to believe in these charms, but as for Mártan, do you suppose he would shave himself on a Monday, for example? Small danger there is of that, in any case, with Sinéad there to stop him!†

The appearance of a simpleton is what Sinéad gives herself day in and day out, stooping under layers of old clothes. You would swear to look at her that she would have a struggle to

---

* *Jaingléir*, a casual fisherman; plural *jaingléirí*.
† Cutting hair, shearing sheep, cutting hay, corn, etc. was not done on a Monday, for it was believed it would bring bad luck.

put one leg in front of the other. But, if you aren't there, it is a different story by her; she will be as fast as Seán Browne's greyhound, and it is the same case with Mártan.

Mártan was never well when he was helping someone else out, but if work for himself is involved, on a day of stacking corn or hay-making, say, there is no hero to match him. But, once he has that done, he will spend a couple of days in bed shamming illness and keeping out of the way of the evil eye. The stale of every ass, the droppings of every dog, and all kinds of old urine are stored away in bottles and old pots by them. But it's worse they are getting lately, for they have a couple of children growing up and they live in mortal dread in case the evil eye falls on them. So, whatever potion or cure is to be found in a goat's udder or the tail of a kid, they will rub it on to them.

Sinéad is the great woman for keeping hens, ducks, and geese and she raises top quality fowl. From east and west the women come running to her in search of good birds. When any fowl belonging to her starts hatching she knocks her off the hatch and sets her laying again.

Yesterday evening a Guard was passing Sinéad's place and this is how the fun began. What did the Guard see but a fine fat goose with a quill stuck across her beak, which made a sorry spectacle of her. The Guard asked about the goose: who owned her, who stuck in the quill and what the reason was. He was told that she belonged to Sinéad and the reason for the quill was to knock her off the hatch. Someone caught the goose for him and he set about removing the quill. As he was pulling it out the goose scattered a load on his uniform that left its mark, and there it will stay for some time to come.

But for that the Guard would hardly have taken the matter of Sinéad and her goose any further. As it is, she has been served with a summons now.

Midday

No day goes by but there is some sport somewhere or other. It is good to have it!

. . . It is said this year that there will be no mackerel in the barrel. A poor prospect. But at the same time people will be as well off. Regarding salt fish, there was never any good in it except that it filled a hole in the guts and that was of course a far cry from hunger.

You don't come across big families in houses these days the same as you used to do, when there were two barrels full of salt fish in the corner as relish with every meal. We have the butcher calling to the door twice a week now and the meat would have to be very poor quality indeed for people not to prefer it to the piece of fish. The farmer that has his wits about him has his own meat; he has put a fine fat pig down in his pickling tub.

A man can have fresh fish for the Friday now for a couple of shillings, his dinner there on a plate. They have, in their own words, Dingle Town in the country now. Even men selling clothes come here from Cork and Limerick, and nothing is more convenient than the article you can buy on the doorstep. All those horses and asses that used to be going the road to Dingle years ago, you never see a sign of them these days.

Philib killed a fine fat pig for himself and his household this very day. That is thirty pounds in money he has saved himself, he declares. Nobody could call this a bad life or anything near it.

Diarmaid Dhonnchadh Begley is after dying in Dingle Hospital today at the age of 80, the tallest man in the barony I suppose, seven feet in height and he well built to match. He had a great command of the Irish language but, as he used to say himself, 'it is neither Irish nor English that ever put a bite on my plate.'

He was a farmer with the grass of one cow and a fisherman too, a fisherman as good as any that ever sat on the thwart of a currach. He spent all his life in the jaws of the waves and often he did not know whether he would come through or whether the crabs would have his corpse. There was no way out of that in the days when Diarmaid was earning his living.

The landing slip from which he used to put to sea was in a bad state, so when the weather broke while he was out it is often he pulled in at Ballydavid. Not that Diarmaid minded, for it gave him an excuse for a pint, something he never refused.

A hero laid low. Eternal rest to his soul!

. . . Murchadh was in with me a short while ago. He was back from Listowel after a visit to Liam Browne who had been on holiday over in Béal Bán here recently. Murchadh spent a night in North Kerry and he was telling me about the time he had and the company. He heard little Gaelic except when Liam and a couple of other men were talking together.

He bought a mare ass there, whatever he wants her for; and if she is two years old she is twenty. He could find nothing under forty pounds but he had no notion that he would have to pay so much for a spindle-shanked ass.

His main thought when he set out was to find a fairly old mare, that with any luck would produce a foal. He is looking out now for a stallion ass somewhere for the mating season in May but, from all he can learn, there is no stallion ass in the barony except one west in Móinteán and another in Coum.

'May the devil sweep Micheál Long too,' says he, 'himself and his lorry! There isn't an ass left in Kerry by him.'

''Tis time for you, Murchadh, to put the asses out of your head and give some thought to yourself.'

'How do you mean "myself"?'

'To find a little mare for yourself.'

'There you go again, the same old tune always by ye. I never met a married man yet but matchmaking was the thought uppermost in his head.'

'All I'm thinking is, if only you had a wife for yourself for the latter end of your days. I don't suppose 'tis any great fist you could make of one now, even if you had her.'

He stared at me. I kept on at him, for I knew my words were not going down too well with him.

'Ah, no, sure 'tis the great time ye have of it, you and your likes. Yourself and your cat, and now the ass. You have no one sticking her nails into you or digging her knees into your rear end in the morning. If you only realized the full truth of the matter, 'tis you are the happiest man under the sun today.'

'How well you didn't stay a gelded dog yourself, for all that!'

'Whisper,' says he to me, and I knew something good was coming from the way he had his eyebrows raised. 'Bod and Com I had here with me for a while last night before they headed for the Captain's house, and do you know what they told me? And I believe them for they are a pair that read newspapers and listen to the wireless.'

'And what did they tell you?'

'They said that anyone with six in the family, or more, would be drawing a big lump of money from now on.'

'That was on the wireless last night.'

'See now, they were right. And if they were, the women will find themselves in the family way during the course of this winter.'

'Didn't that happen when it brought no money to them, only the hunger?'

'It will make a hard year, unless I'm mistaken.'

. . . A hardy, thin, wiry young fellow called in to see me early this morning. Two goats of his, he said, had been driven on to a ledge in the cliff yesterday by dogs; they would never again be able to come up by themselves and his father had told him to come and ask me to rescue them.

'I'll do my best for you,' I said, 'so long as you have rope enough and a good long stick.'

I had my breakfast eaten and my pipe drawing nicely, so I would not be happier going to Windy Gap Fair* than to be setting off to deal with the goats, not that I was overfond of them, for it was often they had made short work of my little cabbage plants. Still, the day of trouble was no time to be drawing that up.

I had six good miles to walk to where the goats were on the ledge. There was plenty of help and I was put in charge of operations. I headed for the cliff with the best of courage for there was no danger involved, though I kept that to myself.

If they had been wild goats they would never have been brought up out of there, for they wouldn't have stayed still until the snares were placed round them. The goat, and the sheep too, must keep still if you are to succeed in slipping the thin rope round the neck. I told the young lad what was to be done, insisting that no move be made after the rope was placed round the neck of the first goat, before the same trick had been performed with the other one.

We had the rods with snares attached and a man in charge of each. One dropped his snare round the head of the older goat and immediately afterwards the other man had the younger goat snared. They had followed orders to work the two rods together. The goats were under control now and all went smoothly. When you saw them clear of danger, the poor things, you would be delighted and be pleased with yourself that you had saved them from death.

* One of the oldest fairs in Ireland, held between Lispole and Leitriúch.

By the same token it was when we had them brought to the cliff top that I thought once more about my little cabbage plants!

There was a public house on our way home and the owner of the goats insisted on taking us in to wet our throats. We left the two goats tethered outside the door and sat down at our ease for ourselves. There was no hurry on us. There never is in a place like that, whatever attraction it has!

Half-way through the first drink we were when in the door came a strong, stout man and a woman in tow by him. Or maybe it was the other way about, for he was an Englishman, to judge from the English he spoke. And so far as they are concerned, those of them we see around here at any rate, it is the wives that wear the breeches and spurs, and do all the riding.

He asked the publican who owned the goats. He told him, in some class of English, about the danger the goats had been in for three days, and how they could not have held out long more only for the men and lads who had faced danger and come to their rescue.

Over to myself the Englishman and his wife came to shake hands, which they did with each of us in turn. He went to the bar, called for a glass of whiskey a man and brought it over to us where we were sitting. When we had our drop swallowed, we had to go out, place all the tackle round the goats that had brought them out of danger, and demonstrate how it had been done. He took photographs of everything, saying he had never seen a plan like it, to snare the two goats at the same time, for fear one of them might jump and go over the cliff. He took great interest in the operation and the shrewdness behind it.

When we went back inside for a parting glass, what the owner of the goats said was that it would be better if they were below on the ledge again tomorrow rather than on the cliff top. Wasn't that a nice way of putting it!

... Tadhg Pheadí from Arda Mór died suddenly yesterday. No one expected it at all and they are wondering what came over him. He was out in the field digging potatoes and he as lively as he ever was. He was not delicate nor was he a man given to complaining of this or that, so the people there are very much shaken by it. There are not many houses in Arda Mór and they don't meet many people. So now with a sudden death in the hamlet they are uneasy over it. Some are saying that death will spare nobody there seeing how it has started like this; with the best man among them picked out first, it must be a poor look-out for others who don't feel too well and have been ailing for a while.

They had a great wake for him, since his death was no great calamity, a man without wife or children. They had lashings of food, drink, and tobacco, and a welcome for everyone who made his way there. If ever there was a proper wake for anybody from the old days till now, it was for poor Tadhg. And there was a funeral to match it on the morning of his burial, as big as if he had been a member of the Irish Parliament.

... It is said that everything has its day. It was very seldom that the people of this barony ever bought coal. They had turf to trample on beneath their feet and it is there still for the cutting.

A glowing fire in every house from morning to night and, on occasion, from night till morning. But that is past and gone, and a new era has come. Faith, people have no fault whatever to find with it, for turf was a great deal of bother and it cost enough too. You lanced out six pounds for a piece of bog before you had the first sod cut. You had to gather a band of turf-cutters and provide food for them, all a lot of fuss and bother, and you needed the right weather too. On top of all that there might be a trudge of five miles to reach the bog.

That was only the first day, and that day might not turn out fine. The band of turf-cutters might often have to spend the whole day working under a steady downpour. Two days had to be spent footing the turf.* Then it could take seven days to draw it home with one horse or two; horseshoes, nails, tackle, and the men themselves—all to see to.

There is expense attached to coal also. It is dear, and the fittings required in the house for burning it are dear. But the benefits and comfort it brings are value for money and people are sure of a glowing fire throughout the year. They did not find it easy of course at first to abandon the old way and adapt themselves to the new, but it won't take long before the new way falls behind the times again. The whole world sloughs its skin.

All-Hallowtide is on top of us again. There are no signs of fine weather at all, only gales of wind from the north-east blowing strong enough to knock the houses down on the poor Christians.

That is not what is troubling people most, for they have grown used to it by now, but what are they going to do without mackerel yellow or green,† something that never happened here before since the Ark came to dry land?

. . . This is All Souls' Day, the day that sends a shiver through the blood, when people are reminded of the dead once more. There are those who never give a thought to the host of the departed until the man with the staff comes along to show them

* Setting it on end in small heaps to dry.
† Mackerel taken from the pickling barrel, washed and left to dry in the sun, attains a yellow hue; when put back for a second pickling it turns green again.

the road, the same as all that went before them. So, don't mention death or the dead to them, just let them row along. All of them are hoping for heaven and running away from the thought of death at the same time. Such is life.

Old people would tell you there was a time when the list of Mass offerings for the dead was never read out from the altar until some bishop or other thought it would be a good plan if the names were read out; it should draw in bags of money. He made a trial of it and another trial. At the third attempt he found he hadn't enough bags to hold all the collection!

Philib of Baile Uí Sheáin used to offer only three shillings so long as his name was not read out before the congregation; many more Philibs besides him offered the same money. But when the names began to be read out, one Philib or other went from three to six shillings and that put the cat among the pigeons.

All the Philibs began cursing one another in turn over offering twice as much for Masses for the dead. This has been going on for some time and nobody knows how far the high-water mark will reach.

The names and the amounts were read out here a while ago and the man who offered only three shillings for the souls of the dead ten years ago has handed in three pounds this year. They say no one ever thought up a better scheme for making money; that it is better by far than the gold mine, for reading out a list of names is little trouble compared to digging underground.

I met Philib's wife on my way home.

'You were listening to the list of offerings for the dead being read out this morning, I suppose,' I said to her.

'I was, dear heart,' says she, 'and what do a couple of shillings like that matter once a year? If they were alive, sure, wouldn't it cost twelve times as much to keep them in food and tobacco. And there's something else you must remember, didn't some of them leave pennies behind?'

Says I to myself, when she had gone her way, Bríde would have made a good lawyer. Or maybe a fine fat bishop was lost in her! Eoghan Rua was right, if he it was that said: 'The black raven has not yet learnt speech.'*

. . . Today is Sunday and I went to ten o'clock Mass, the regular Mass for the public. I notice a custom creeping in here these days—the Mass for the public is being offered up for the soul of somebody departed, whose name is read from the altar. I do not agree with this, nor do many more besides me. If it is Mass for the public, let it be the public's Mass. If it is for the dead, then it should be a separate Mass, said specially for the dead. But this is killing two birds with one stone.

That is not all of it, though. The Priest gave a new sermon today. He was giving out about constantly crying poverty—'the poor mouth'—and how it was driving people out of the country; the end result would be houses all over the place left bleak and empty. The sign of a degenerate race, that's what 'the poor mouth' was, he declared. ' "Fortune favours the brave", isn't that what ye say often yeerselves, as yeer people did before ye. And it is a lack of courage and hope that is the cause of "the poor mouth".' And so on.

That is only part of the story, although he was right in a way. Which is worse, does he think, 'the poor mouth' or real poverty? There was a time when there was no call for 'the poor

* The famous eighteenth-century Kerry Gaelic poet and wit Eoghan Rua O'Sullivan was in the company of a priest when a raven flew by. The priest asked, jokingly, when would the raven learn speech. Eoghan instantly replied:

> When the whale comes up to the moorland,
> When France extends to Slieve Mish,
> When thirst for gold has left the priest,
> The raven will then have learnt speech.

mouth'. A man and his wife would sit down to the table surrounded by six or seven children, and they having only the bare potatoes with nothing to savour them often enough. Do not God and man know that that couple had no need to say a word? Wasn't 'the poor mouth' the picture the children saw in front of them on the table?

But, thanks be to God, that life is gone. I was talking with an old man a couple of days ago who is well over the 80. He's the man that remembers the picture on the table, when his mother used to dry the tea leaves so as to put them down to draw again, and again too maybe. And, if people have 'the poor mouth' in the life that's in it today, maybe that's no bad sign, a sign only that their lot has improved and they feel that things will be better still. It is no bad sign to hear people airing their grievances. Putting up with things in total silence is worse.

... Bod and Com went fishing last night again. It was the currach they took out, with another *jaingléir* at the stern. So, there is a fair amount of fish in the village today and you can smell the mackerel grilling in every house. No fish reached Murchadh, I fancy, and if so there will be ructions over it. Certainly, when I was walking westwards past his house—and it was Murchadh's breakfast time—I suspected it was the hen's egg he was having for it. If it had been mackerel, the smell would have reached me.

There are those, however, who would tell you that Murchadh tosses any fish that comes his way to the cat. He has no mind for it himself and never ate a bite of fish in his life, for he does not know how to grill it properly. Also, that laziness would not let him put it down to boil. But, let fish come to the village and, if Murchadh doesn't get one, there is red war over it.

So, if he was given no mackerel today, there will be sport at the 'Well' tonight, for the two fishermen will catch it properly from Murchadh. 'A child covets whatever he sees,' as the old saying goes.

Proof has been given to all the others by Bod and Com that the fish are there for the catching. The big boats are lying idle, however, moored beside the slipway and rings of rot beginning to appear on them for lack of use. It is the crews of the currachs that will prove their worth yet even though the day of the currach is over, and what a blessing that is!

The Captain called in today around the time for sitting down to the potatoes. It was easily known that last night's mackerel catch would nag at him. It is with him Bod and Com go out fishing when he unmoors the boat, and they are the crew he prefers to have. But, when dealing with mackerel, it is good to have the fourth man along, and I knew well that he wanted me to go with them; it was what brought him.

'The weather does not look too promising,' I said, 'to go out at all.'

'How well the two devil-may-cares faced out last night and how well it was not empty-handed they came back. They brought in one and a half thousand mackerel, by my baptism.'

'For the one cast of the nets, I was told.'

'The one cast and make for port.'

'But you would be going further out to sea.'

'If so, haven't I the boat and tackle for it; and the help if they come along? Yerra, strike your hand across your heart and make your way northwards. I don't think it will be a bad night and we'll make a run out.'

I knew of course that he had a drop taken; otherwise he would not be half so eager. I gave him my promise to go to sea with him so long as he found someone else; that we might as well be there for part of the night as anywhere else.

'I'll call on Bod and Com on my way home now,' says he,

'and there's little fear but they will be there when you come. Waiting for the wind of the word is all they are; wasn't that what took them out last night? And fish or no fish, all that pair ever want is an excuse to be in the village; any place where there are two public houses.'

Five o'clock came round and a trip to sea seemed a better prospect than to be lying there stretched on the couch. There was no great strain involved in the work, with a good sea-worthy boat powered by an engine and no stroke to do other than casting the nets and hauling them in at your ease.

When I arrived at the harbour my boat was afloat and the nets on board, for those two boyos had been in the village for the past couple of hours. 'Yes,' says I to myself, '"Where there's a will there's a way,"' and I knew well that the pair of them had washed the salt out of their teeth by then.

A man standing further up called down to me that all was ready and we would be sailing at any time. I sauntered along up and when I rounded the corner what should I hear but fine music being expertly played.

I put my head in at the door of the public house and there I saw my Bod playing; my Com was pounding the floor and he had even flung his cap aside. The Captain was there himself and says he to me, 'Well, what have you to say now?'

'The devil a thing have I to say except 'tis a great pity everyone in Ireland isn't like them.'

Com had every whoop out of him and wasn't Bod the man able to drive him wild!

'Here,' says the Captain to me, 'drink up that pint and we'll be away.'

Bod heard him. 'Yerra, the devil sweep you, wouldn't I be over in Newfoundland at that rate before night falls?' The last thought in Bod's head was to stir out of there until everybody else left too!

'Whisper, Captain,' says myself, 'have you the lamps ready yet?'

'No, nor have I any drop to put in them.' With that he calls one of the publican's young sons and tells him to fill a bottle for him for the lamps.

'Will you look at those two harum-scarums,' says he to me, 'that are here since two o'clock today. 'Tis little thought they give to lamp or light, or anything except filling their bellies with porter and nothing in their heads but music and dancing.'

'Haven't we done a good job?' says Bod, and he playing away all the while. 'We have boat and nets in full order, so there's nothing to do but jump on board.' Words were falling from Bod's lips now which I do not need to repeat here. Suffice it to say that if the Captain was not the butt of abuse from Bod and Com, no man ever was. But he was never one to take offence at what anyone said, so long as he had his crew, the very men he wanted.

I drank my pint measure at my ease and had just emptied it when Bod ordered a refill for me and two more pints to go with it. 'Only the one will be drawn now,' said the Captain. 'Ye have yeer fill of it. Ye are putting to sea and ye'll get no more drink.'

'Yerra, Great God of Glory! the drop of it I've swallowed wouldn't last me out as far as Gob Point,'* says Bod.

'Fill up the pints,' I said myself, for I knew that however much drink my pair had down them they would show no sign of it the moment they set foot in the boat; they are two real craftsmen when it comes to pints, boats, or the sea; a pair without flaw or fault.

Time to go came and away we went to sea, the Captain at the helm and the three of us lying sprawled on the nets. It is no use trying to talk when this boat is travelling, for the engine

* On the Great Blasket Island.

makes too much noise. The tide was ebbing fast by the time the Captain had steered east from Streall. When the tip of Mount Brandon came into view we stopped and cast the nets. We struck the match and were smoking a fine plug of tobacco for ourselves; the weather was perfect by this time and no fear on anyone nor any occasion of it there either. If ever we left the nets down for a long spell it was that night.

Bod was lilting away. The 'Dingle Races' was the name of the tune, he said. The Captain called from behind saying fish were going into the nets.

'Ah, what else, man,' says Bod, 'don't you know that when I strike up my tune I set the fish dancing and this is not the first night I've done it.'

'The devil a fish am I aware of,' said Com, 'and 'tis strange how I wouldn't notice anything stirring as well as the next man.'

'Blast and sweep you, Com, up there!' cried the Captain, 'you with your lugholes stuffed full with the froth of porter; as if you would notice anything!'

'Himself is on the "teat" back there unbeknownst to anybody,' Bod said in a whisper to myself. 'Didn't you notice the noggin being slipped into the locker before you left? He's there taking swigs of it ever since we lowered the nets.'

The words were no sooner out of his mouth than we heard all the thrashing about in the sea below us and saw the water shooting into the air.

'There now,' says the Captain, 'what did I tell ye? If we have caught a heavy fish, we won't bring half our nets away with us.'

'There's no fish there,' I said. 'No fish would send the sea shooting up like that. You have something else. A huge sea-animal is caught in the nets and if he is tangled up in them you can bid them goodbye.'

All the spirit drained out of Bod and Com as soon as I mentioned the word 'sea-animal'. We started to haul in the nets but we saw no mackerel, not a single fish. We had two of the nets on board when the animal gave another heave, sending the spray flying up over the side of the boat on top of us. When the Captain saw the floundering in the water he got a fright, for he had never come up against a sea-animal before.

Bod did have some experience of them, so coping with this one did not greatly bother him. We were hauling away until we came to the last net. It was in this that the laddo had been caught. There was no word out of the Captain behind.

'Whisper,' says Bod to myself, 'where is all his great swearing now? Isn't it good that everyone meets his master and wasn't this sea-animal sorely needed tonight? I prefer to have him than ten pounds' worth of fish in the nets, though 'tis sorely I need the pennies.'

When Com saw there was no dread on us over the animal he pulled himself together and found fresh courage. That is the kind of man he is; he would never let it be said that anything would cause him fear or dread. We hauled in until we had the animal alongside and, so far as we could make out, he had died in the nets, but caution held us back from taking a chance on it. Since we had the big boat, we were not half so afraid of him.

'Have a word with himself,' I said to Bod, 'and find out if we are to tow the animal home.' Bod asked him.

'Use your knife on the net in the name of the God of Glory,' came the answer.

'Upon my soul,' said Bod, 'when he's in a tight corner, or terror grips him, 'tis then he knows the Man above is there.'

'Quick, cut the net free, Com!' the Captain shouted from behind. 'There's an ugly bank of black cloud gathering west of me and I'll see if I can make port before it breaks.'

The knife edge was put to the net and we said goodbye for

ever to the sea-animal. The Captain was aft at the helm, mad
with rage, and he letting fly every swear at the animal and
ourselves. He pointed the boat landwards and we hauled out
our pipes. We were able to take our ease on the journey home,
though we had nothing to show for our night's work but
misfortune, God help us! It was not the first night this
happened to us or to others like us, but as the saying goes,
'Life at sea is cheerless' and that is not due to the cold
altogether but because the entire business is bleak and
dispiriting.

Bod spoke up when it dawned on him where the prow of the
boat was heading.

'What's wrong with the devil back there,' he said, 'or where
does he mean to go?'

The boat was zigzagging in her course at this time, now
heading back to port, now heading out to sea, and nobody in
charge of her. Com called to the Captain but if he did he
received no answer from him. He rushed aft and what was it
but my man stretched out cold, and not even drawing breath.

'My heart to the devil,' he shouted to Bod, 'come back here
quick, he's out cold!'

Back rushed Bod and I'd say it knocked no great start out of
him to find the Captain lying there stiff and cold. He placed his
hand on him and found that he had gone stone cold. 'Seán,
boy,' says he, 'this fellow has passed away, so what are we to
do?'

I went to have a look. 'Lift him out on to the nets,' I advised,
'and I'll say an Act of Contrition into his ear. There is breath in
him still and if he is to depart this life, so be it.'

We lifted him forward, rubbing him hard and vigorously and,
on my soul, when he felt the sea water on his head, it was soon
he stirred. When Bod saw him drawing breath, he owned that
he would spend another day in his own house. 'Upon my

soul, boy,' says he, 'dealing with a sea-animal is nothing compared to a human animal.'

'Shake him well now,' I said to Bod. 'We can take him back to the locker, for maybe he hasn't drunk it all yet and another drop may do him good. He is very cold still.'

'May God forbid, wisha! Isn't that what has him in his present state? Leave it where it is, I say.'

'Never mind that. If he managed to reach port alive we would have got ourselves out of a tangle, and some of us would be finished with him for the rest of his days.'

I went back to see if he had left any drop which I could rub on to him. 'There is no drop here,' says Com, 'no more than there is in the hole of the thole-pin, but I'd say there's a bottle around with the smell of petrol from it.'

'Can you put your hand on it for me?'

'I don't know where it is now, for I'm knocked all of a heap by that son of a whore since I found him laid out a while ago.'

'Yerra, take no notice of a man that collapses like that. Don't people faint inside the chapel? He is coming round now, and if I had that bottle with the petrol in it I'd make a man of him.'

Com searched the locker and faith he found it. I switched on the torch and examined my bottle; it was a good half-empty. It was not petrol, though, but the methylated spirit he had for lighting the lamp. I went forward and rubbed it on to his chest and back. Bod took over the rubbing and before long the Captain uttered his first word.

'The curse of God on you,' said Bod, 'if it isn't you that has me at the end of my tether!'

He came to himself at a bound and the devil's own wonder on him over where he was. He said he thought he was in bed dreaming about the sea-animal and how all his nets had been lost.

We were not far from the harbour now and we well satisfied

with the night. We had set one animal adrift and had another animal on board with us, but he was alive and talking! We sailed in and all was put to rights, with the boat secured at anchor and the nets on the quay.

'Whisper now, men,' says Bod, 'let no one make for the public house above yet, until we see what he does. Let everyone pretend he's making for his own cabin.'

That is what we did. Every ass has his own trickery and, when the Captain turned west, we faced south, bidding him 'goodnight'. He let an almighty roar out of him. 'Where do ye think ye're going? 'Pon my own soul there's no home for ye for a while yet, whatever. Give a few knocks on the door of the 'Well' above, for ye must have a thirst on ye after the night. The man there will let ye in, have no fear, so long as ye have me at yeer back.'

We had no great longing for it, we let on, but the thirst of the dying was on Com and he said he would have to give up play-acting, or it might go too far. We went into the pub.

It was no porter the Captain would give us, the poor man, but a drop of the red stuff, brandy or whiskey, he didn't care which.

The crack was in full spate and we drinking away at our ease. There was no thought in anybody's head of going home at all, so we made a night of it till morning. 'Stay aboard here now,' Bod said to me, 'for no animal will come here to bother you, though it wasn't the sea-animal that caused us the most trouble but the land-animal!'

By now it was past midnight, nearer to day than to night and, when fishermen are out overnight and have not returned by the expected time, their people at home are thrown into a panic. We knew well that as soon as day brightened the hounds would be out on our trail. And we knew only too well, on top of this, that our wives would be after our blood. But we had resigned ourselves to accepting whatever punishment they had in mind for us; we would make the most of our solace from the glass.

Bod takes hold of the melodeon and strikes up the 'Liverpool Hornpipe'. In no time Com is step-dancing away, and pounding the floor like mad. What harm if he had a step in him but he hadn't, only the drink gone to his head and he must be making a show of himself.

Now and again Bod would stop playing and tell him that he was a step or two out of time with the music and would have to start again.

'Strike up the music and play away like the devil,' says Com, 'what does it matter to us only to be whiling away the night.'

'Amn't I telling you that you're out of step with the music and what's the use in playing for you? Wouldn't a mule dance it better for me?'

'Not at all, 'tis how you can't play to the steps I'm dancing. 'Tis rare steps I have, boy, that ye never saw in this village.'

'I don't know,' said Bod to me in the heel of the hunt, 'but do you think we will have to put him away or will he go to the madhouse of his own accord?'

We all burst out laughing and it seemed the Captain would collapse. We were as merry as crickets until there came a knock on the door and the bailiffs were in on top of us!

It was the furthest thought from our minds by this time that the bailiffs would be coming for us. We were guilty and convicted of the offence and we knew it. All we could do was hold steady against the wind and take whatever they let fly at us. Our three wives they were and it was Bod's wife who was first in the door and spoke her piece:

'May neither God nor Mary come to yeer help anyway! If my heart isn't crossways over ye ever since five o'clock this morning and I thinking the crabs were chewing the nozzles off ye out there at the bottom of the sea! Bad scran and bad cess to yeer like, if it isn't snug and happy ye are and other people in torment and trouble over ye!'

They set about driving us out the door but, upon my soul, they failed in the attempt for we were full of Dutch courage by this time.

'Yerra, my good woman,' says Bod, because, I suppose, it was his own wife that had spoken, 'aren't we alive and what more do ye want? Why don't ye wait for an explanation and put a question over what happened to us?'

They would neither question nor talk to us, nor would they give us any hearing at all. They only wanted us to clear out and go home. The plan Bod adopts then is to pick up the melodeon once more and make the women listen to the music. Com takes hold of my own 'Queen' and hauls her out on to the floor. The next thing he knows is that she has sent him flying seven feet away and he is lying there all of a heap on the floor!

I caught hold of Bod's wife myself and swung her round, and round again, in step with the music. She stayed dancing with me until we were both exhausted. By this time the Captain had thought of another shift. He had seen to it that a drop of punch was prepared for the women and they drank it back.

'Let ye be thankful,' said he, 'that these good men are alive after this night,' and he related all that had happened from start to finish.

They calmed down when they heard the Captain telling about the hardship of the night and how we had weathered it and come through. It was the last night of the fishing season for us, as the Captain told them, and says he, 'We must not complain over what we have made out of it. And by the same token we must not be faulted for giving it a good send-off tonight.'

We set off home, taking our leave of the Captain, three men with their garnish of women at eight o'clock in the morning, and farmers going to the creamery with their milk. Philib came towards us with his own tank and says he, knowingly: 'I thought Puck Fair* was a long way off still.'

'Ah,' says Bod, 'it will last a full week this year, for tinkers are after travelling there from Newfoundland and a good show must be put on for them.'

'Or is it from the Festival of Tralee† ye're coming? I thought at first 'twas the Roses ye were bringing back with ye!'

'Aren't you aware,' says Bod, 'that these women here have skin as smooth from the navel as any Rose at all that was ever raised in Tralee?'

That put an end to the morning's work and we went to sleep for ourselves. We had it well earned.

. . . When I got up I strolled west towards the village, for no day passes but you meet with some entertainment or company there. I met Máire Bhuí from the lower end of the parish north of us. She was coming back after collecting the pension for herself and her husband. She has great faith in me, I don't know why.

'The old lad at home is not good for some while,' she told me. 'He's complaining that his bladder and his gut are not working properly.'

'Why don't you fetch the doctor to him?'

'To him is it? Fetch the doctor to him, are you saying? I pity your head! Sure he would only shoot the doctor and he'd make you suffer for it then. I'm trying to cure him myself this while past but, on my soul, my medicines aren't working too well for me, and I find that strange. I gave him a dose for the bladder

* Annual fair and carnival in August in Killorglin, Co. Kerry, when a puck goat is crowned as King of the Fair.
† Rose of Tralee beauty contest and festival, also in August.

yesterday and only for the drop of brandy I happened to have in the house I'd say they would be putting nails in his coffin today. When he had got over the upset he lay back and I gave him my solemn promise not to give the dose again. I don't know what I'll do with him now.'

'And are his bowels working at all?'

'Not without taking this dose. He has trouble passing water too, but I'm not worrying over that, for the cure I have for it is working. It is the gut that is more serious for him now.'

'There's only one thing you can do with him and that is whip him off to the hospital where everyone goes that has anything serious wrong with him. If he is going to get any better, that is where it will happen.'

'O my dear,' she said to me pitifully, 'I couldn't bear to part with him, for I'm too wrapped up in him.'

I strolled on west homewards after taking my leave of her. I swallowed a bite and told my own 'Queen' about Máire's troubles. Her comment was that Liam was not robust enough to fight off an ailment like that. While we were talking a little girl came to the door, all in a lather after coming on her bicycle to tell us her grandad was dying.

The news came as no great surprise to me. I went and picked up a little book that contained the Litanies in Irish. I put it in my pocket saying to the 'Queen' that it was strange, and mighty strange, for a devil to be setting out to read the Litanies over an angel!

I jumped on my bicycle and when I reached Liam's place he was drawing his last breath. I started reading and had just come to the end of the Litanies when poor Liam was on the road to eternity.

The little girl gazed at him and says she: 'Look, he is alive still, his eyes are open!'

'That is death's way with many people, girl,' said Máire

Bhuí, 'it opens their eyes for them. There is a big long road ahead of him and if death closed his eyes he could not find his way.'

I said the prayer for the dead for his soul and left them, for I knew they had enough to help without me. And I knew there would be a wake over Liam according to the old custom, a wake lasting two days and two nights. These are humble folk that would not break with the tradition of a two days' wake except where death was a very great calamity, which in Liam's case it was not, only an angel going home for himself after the share of purgatory he suffered in this life.

. . . I have spent part of the night at the wake-house and, I swear on my solemn oath, I would rather be listening to the cross-talk there than in the Irish Parliament. It was an old man's wake, so everybody could have his say. But I had one fault to find with it—too many women were there and wherever that is the case, it is no small drawback.

Dónall Mhártan was there. If Dónall hears word of a wake anywhere throughout the length and breadth of Corcaguiny* he makes sure to attend. It is mostly to fill his belly with porter that Dónall turns up.

When twelve o'clock strikes, all go on their knees to say the Rosary for the Dead, but when some fellows have a drop taken it is during the Rosary they generally start up their devilment. You never see clay pipes at any wake nowadays; the tobacco is sliced on to a plate and you can be filling your own pipe away for yourself. So, since they can't have the clay pipes, it leaves the playboys with nothing to hurl at people during the Rosary. That was not the case this night, though, for they had filled

* The Dingle Peninsula.

their pockets with clods of turf, waiting for the moment to start pelting.

The first decade had only just been said when a good hard clod struck Dónall right across the ear but, faith, he never let on. There were sniggers from this side and sniggers from that at Dónall and, when the first shot didn't knock any stir out of him, a second one caught him below the temple.

'Wisha, the devil fire ye, that ye wouldn't give over yeer blackguarding, or is there no fear of God on ye at all?' says he. Beit, his wife, was sitting in the corner and she it was that the next clod struck and, if it did, she crossed over to the corner opposite.

The Rosary was nearly said and the time for pelting over, but there are those that never know when enough is enough. One of the blackguards had a couple of clods of turf left and I suppose he wanted to go one better than everyone else. He had more than his share of drink taken and what did he do but let fly at poor Liam, the corpse laid out, and hit him in the forehead.

His widow Máire turned on them viciously and venomously saying that the person who threw the clod at the corpse would be a corpse himself before the morrow was out. Nobody had a word to say after this outburst and it was the quiet of the dead with us surely for some while.

Dónall Mhártan was a target no longer and he addressed the man laid out beside him: 'Yerra, wisha, we must make allowances for the young. If their like weren't there, wouldn't we be lost without them? And 'tis hard to put a wise head on young shoulders.'

With that the bucket of porter circulated again and soon everything settled down. The fear they had of Máire faded, and of her curses in the presence of the dead.

Máire came up to me on the day of the funeral, the day after the morrow. What was troubling her, she said, was that it was herself who brought on Liam's death with her purgatives and cures, and that if she had sent him to the hospital he might be alive still. 'He was above ground yesterday,' says she, 'and we have him under it today.'

'That is what is fated for us, Máire, so be saying your prayers for his soul,' I said to her.

... My regular habit is to leave my abode here each evening and walk as far as Ballynalackan. No day goes by but you will meet some devil or other who will while away part of it for you, some of them having nothing else to do, for it is on the dole they are depending, the poor creatures.

I was nearing the village when I heard an old woman giving out, and with a torrent of Irish that would have left Father Peadar O'Leary standing any day.* The old woman, though, was not so mild and gentle in her language as O'Leary would have been, nor so polite. But it was the stream of curses from her I was eager to hear because I'm sick of the prayers. And another point, when some of these old people are lying under the clay all this flow of language will be lost to us for good, though the prayers will be left, I suppose.

What happened was that two cocks had gone for each other's crests and a big fight had taken place. The old woman owned one of them and he was lying there, almost at his last gasp, when she found him. The other cock had crossed over the boundary into her yard and she took the matter up from there.

I drew close, fearing I might miss any of the 'grammar' she was letting fly.

She stooped down to pick up her own cock and just then a

---

* Well-known Gaelic scholar and writer, author of *My Own Story* (Oxford, 1988).

gust of wind blew from behind that lifted every stitch of clothing up over her head. If so, it was little the notice she took of it, or myself either.

She picked up her cock and out the gate she went, striding east towards the house of the woman that owned the other cock, Joan Thomáis. 'Come out here to me, you great bitch, till you see what your thieving cock has done to mine!'

Joan stepped out to face her and she well prepared for her, because she had a good notion she would be on the warpath.

'Shame and disgrace to you anyhow, if it isn't you have the nerve to come to my doorstep on a wild evening instead of staying at home for yourself! You could be combing your hair and shaking your shirt* over the fire and not be going all round the village, scratching yourself against the gateposts . . .'

Before Joan knew what was happening the other woman had given her a clout across the side of the head with the cock she was holding. They were letting words fly at each other now that have never been heard in a sermon yet. Joan picked herself up, and wherever she kept her blackthorn stick she used it to beat the other woman about the ears, leaving her sprawled on the heap of manure. It wasn't long though before she was up again asking for a second blow of the stick and she got it quick and smart.

The old woman gave a terrible scream that her skull was split in two, and she could be heard all over the village.

'Clear off home for yourself, you dirty old rip!' said Joan. 'Your blood is spilling from you, so lick it and find out what it tastes like; for too long I've kept my patience with you, but thanks be to God the day has dawned when I don't need to put up with you any longer and I have cleared you from the door.'

The old woman wasn't worth three halfpence going home

---

* To shake fleas off.

after the bout. I returned to my own abode with a story to relate. Soon after my tea a Guard came to the house investigating what happened. 'It was easily known,' says I to myself, 'that I would pay for the evening, if I have to go to court as a witness about these two after my day.' It was no more than I deserved I suppose, seeing that I didn't turn on my heel when the trouble started. But that would have been too much to expect of any man.

. . . There are days now and again when men come to the forge and the blacksmith is nowhere to be found, for he has the seven cares of the mountain on his shoulders besides the work of the forge.

I found Philib there before me when I called in today which suited me fine, for I could be letting fly at him out of my store and he not caring whether it was truth or fancy. And I'm not sure, for all his innocent airs, but it is stringing me along that devil is often. You can't read him in some ways. The blacksmith wasn't there so we started chatting until he came.

'I have three or four cows above,' he said, 'that will not keep the service of the bull. They will drive me out of house and home unless a remedy can be found.'

'And whose bull do you take them to?'

'I don't take them to anyone.'

'Don't tell me 'tis the creamery bull that services them for you?'

'It is so, wisha, and I'm not very thankful to him.'

'Haven't you heard, Philib, that 'tis the modern method from America people use now?'

'Ah, God save us always, I hope it isn't true. What I maintain is that there's nothing like the old way and nothing will convince me otherwise. It would not be easy to better the old custom.'

With that a man came in looking for the blacksmith, or where was he at all?

'He's not far from you,' Philib told him. 'He's behind there in the shed and he guiding his boar to mount a sow.'

'He's the great man,' says this fellow, 'that can master every craft.'

The blacksmith came in bristling, for he knew there would be men waiting for him.

'There you are,' said the stranger, but the blacksmith did not answer. He only made a grab at the bellows and started working it on the fire in the hearth, until he was sending sparks flying all over the forge and smoke billowing up the chimney. He thrust a couple of bars of iron in the fire and when they were reddened enough he lifted them out on to the anvil.

A third man arrived outside the forge, a man who had not stepped inside it for half a century, I suppose, until now. He had left the district as a youngster and gone over to America. He had little schooling beyond knowing four from five when he planted his feet in the land across. He buckled to and brought a big lump of money home out of there. Music or carousing never tempted him, but as he earned the dollar he locked it away.

This man spent forty-five years working in a rubber works and he never felt the years go by until he was told it was time to retire. The size of the lump sum they gave him on top of the pension came as a complete surprise. It was then the fit took him to come back home and spend the remainder of his days in his native place.

No light was put out for a week in Ballynalackan when Tadhg came home. All were invited, strangers and relations alike, and he left no thirst on them during that week. But however high the tide the ebb comes, and so it was with Tadhg's nights. He had to call a halt and all was at an end.

He started visiting the public house regularly then, and if he didn't find a bright welcome there! Some were saying it was God that sent him to them. It was true for them!

That was Tadhg's practice for a couple of months and, I own to you, an eye was kept out for him to see in which direction he might be heading as soon as he put his foot over the threshold. If he faced west the look-out was off calling the stokers. They had it neatly worked out between them that they would stroll in at intervals in twos, so that the round of drinks Tadhg would call for might not be out of the way. The ploy was working fine for a while, but what is there that lasts for ever? It did not take long before the stokers were shovelling deep and emptying the coal out of Tadhg's pockets. He was forced to change tack.

There was no other remedy now but to give up the company for a while; this is what he did, for the coal would not last, with stokers in there with him who knew their trade.

He came into the forge and I asked him where he was spending his nights now, as I no longer saw him west.

'*Chrissake, man,*'* he said, 'where can you turn and the cats of the village keeping a look out for you? Or, do they think I don't understand what's going on? I understand well, *goddam it*.† I know they were taking advantage of me, but when I had the drop taken I was past caring. There was nothing for it at last but to draw the boat up on dry land altogether and stow away the nets. For 'tis only worse they would be getting and you would have the same thanks for it in the end.'

'I suppose you are finished with the place across, Tadhg.'

'*Goddam sure,*‡ I am. I spent a long term in America, and to be

---

* In English in the original.
† English.
‡ English.

back here in Ireland is worth more to me than half of all the money I ever earned over there. I feel young again since I came home.'

'You will push the boat out again.'

'I will surely, but the cats will have to be brought under control first.'

'The cats will find some other simpleton, never fear.'

I left them there and went home. The blacksmith never uttered so much as a word all the while.

. . . Middle-aged men have nowhere else to go now to while away part of the night except the public house. You won't find anybody going to the 'gathering house' these days or listening to the weaving of stories as in times gone by. If a man launched into a tale—and let him be the finest story-teller that ever put a foot in a boot—the place would soon be as empty as the chapel.

In this way many relics of the past are disappearing. Somehow a new era begins every sixty years in the cycle of life, and that change causes the rift between young and old, so it is the case that we no longer understand each other. This is the common experience; it is not mine alone.

The priest was giving a sermon from the altar today according to Luke and Mark, and nobody paying any heed to him. He might as well have been preaching about two asses from Listowel for all the difference it made. And nothing of this escapes him, for it is only too well he has the congregation sized up. Let him bring up the next life to people nowadays who care for little else except the things of this life and he would be better off leaving it unsaid. The result is that most of the old ways are gone to eternity, and maybe that is where some of them ought to be.

If things go on as they are, soon the public house will end up being the chapel for them. There the old way of life and the new are on the same ground, living side by side every night. It is the one place now where young and old meet together to while away part of the night in each other's company. The only other place where that happens is the chapel and they don't all talk to each other there.

There is no subject whatever that is not discussed openly when the drop of drink heats the blood in a man, for he is no longer the same person then. There was Murchadh himself last night and he well loosened because he has no great head for the drink and it is easy to heat the blood in him. We were comparing the old ways to the new and it is well he puts things at times, although he is a man that never bothered his head much with schooling.

'Do you note the great changes that have taken place in your lifetime?' he asked.

'I note them surely. Why wouldn't I?'

'Are you aware that it isn't the same life at all that was there when you were young?'

'But it is a change for the better.'

'I don't know, the devil take me, wisha! Good men sacrificed their lives over half a century ago* but that was not for the life we see around us today. To take only the Irish language itself for an instance, look at that wireless set there in the corner and all I ever hear coming out of it is English, after all the blood that was shed against it. And listen to the songs being sung around you at times.'

'But the two ways of life have to be there; the one puts the other to the test. Isn't that how it has always been in this country, Murchadh?'

'Look,' he said, 'Queen Elizabeth of England did more for us in her day, although it wasn't for our good maybe, or our

---

* In the Easter Rising, 1916 and the subsequent War of Independence.

way of life. But see what she did for us with the Brindled Cat.*
Sure it gave our people knowledge of how to read and write
Irish the first day ever. Where would we be if we had to depend
on our own people to do that for us?'

'There is much in what you say, do you know that? And
here's another thing, I am sure if she came around today with
all her pots, no one would go without soup or gruel, whatever
they might have to renounce for it.'†

'Isn't there greater respect today for the stock of the people
who dipped their heads into the pot than there is for you or
me? Wasn't that what started me off in the first place?'

'I remember,' I said to him, 'a period in life, and I a
youngster on the Blasket, when there were old women there
who had never read a book or a history in their lives; when you
recall what they were saying during those times, it would give
you cause for serious thought today. I recall one of them, a
mother of ten children, who had little coming in; it was during
the fighting in Dublin and news reached us from Dunquin that
a man was dying on hunger strike. What she said was, "The
poor foolish man that wouldn't eat the food while he has it to
eat. Someone else will eat it with relish when he is gone and
forgotten entirely." Look at that for shrewdness from a woman
without any learning.'

'Didn't you hear what the old man above here said, whose
sons had served time in one prison after another for their
country; when he saw the changes taking place today he said,

* John O'Kearney's *Catechism* was the first book printed in Gaelic, by order of
Queen Elizabeth in 1571. There is confusion here because the *Brindled Cat* is a
reference to nineteenth-century proselytizing classes to teach Gaelic speakers to
read the Bible. Simple primers were used with sentences such as *Tá an cat
breac*—'the cat is brindled'.
† Queen Elizabeth I is used here to stand for proselytizing Protestant missionaries
who distributed soup and gruel at times of scarcity and famine during the
nineteenth century.

and he put it well, boy, "The boar's backside to his own litter."
And wasn't he absolutely right, when you look round at what's
happening today?'

'"The boar's backside to his own litter"—that was a striking
way he put it; and he was right.'

We changed the subject. 'Whisper, Murchadh, it is not all
that often indeed you call here. I come far more often. But tell
me this much, what brings you here?'

'To take my mind off troubles, wisha, and come away from
the misery for a while. When I take two drinks I am satisfied.
But, if I got the third drink, I own to you I wouldn't care if I
stayed till morning, if they let me.'

'I wonder whether 'tis that brings Tadhg from Ballynalackan
here, do you think?'

'It is not. The man with his wits about him is not to be
compared to the madman, whose coming here is the same as
going to the madhouse for a spell. He and his likes never come
to their senses entirely until they have spent that while here.
Tadhg is in his right mind again now.'

. . . On the previous day I had taken my stroll to Ballynalackan
as is usual for me of an evening. I was just heading into the
village when I saw two goats and a pair of fine hardy kids with
them, the kids on top of a fence-wall and the mothers trying to
clamber up to them. There were fetters on the goats, but these
would be no great bar to their nimbleness when they took the
notion to jump.

The kids jumped over the fence as soon as they caught sight
of me and, with that, the mothers followed swiftly and easily. I
am forever hearing that, if you come across the devil anywhere,
the shape he has is the goat with the horns. They were not long
inside the fence when the owner of the cabbage garden came
along, clapped eyes on them at once and in he went after them

in an almighty temper. He punched and pushed the big goats and threw them out into the road, on top of each other.

'Mártan,' says I to him, speaking for his own good, 'don't go any further now with your thumping, for maybe you would kill one of them, and if you do, 'tis you will pay for it.'

'The slaughter of the Dún on them!'* he said, 'and on the man that owns them! I'm driven clean out of my wits by them and if they continue plaguing me they will drive me to the Glen of the Mad. This is not their first or second time doing it, but every cursed day of the week. There's no remedy for it only the law.'

I was telling all this to Murchadh when he happened to glance over his shoulder and said: 'Look who's coming in now as bad luck would have it!'

Who was it but the owner of the goats.

I bethought myself, knowing that many a man walks into a place like this and he is not in the same humour leaving it as he was coming. A great deal of poison comes out with the froth of the porter. He had a couple of drinks and then came across to me.

'You were watching Mártan of the Shit blackguarding my goats last night,' he said. 'Are you aware that he left one of them dead?'

'If I was,' I said, 'I saw no goat being killed, as you make out. And isn't it mighty sure you are that I was there, or what witness have you that I was?'

I had these words barely out of my mouth when who should walk in the door but Mártan himself, and I fancied that he

---

* Dún an Óir, a fort on the West Kerry coast, was captured by Queen Elizabeth's forces under Lord Grey during a rebellion in 1580. The poet Edmund Spenser was present as Grey's secretary and it is believed that Sir Walter Raleigh carried out the execution of the garrison of 600. His name was used locally into the present century to quieten or frighten children.

caught something of what I said. He ordered a glass of whiskey and tossed it back. But, for fear Mártan had not heard me, I went on:

'Name your witness now. Whoever told you I saw one of your goats being killed yesterday told you a lie.'

The man of the goats was pulling in his horns ever since he became aware that Mártan had arrived, and had a glass of whiskey in his belly now. I was gathering confidence from the way he was acting and I past caring at all by this time. That is how drink takes even the best of us. Mártan turned round. The drop of the hard stuff was beginning to take effect.

'What goats?' he asked. A hush fell on all there, for they had scented what was in the wind from listening to myself and the owner of the goats.

'What goat was killed?' He was like a bull gone berserk.

'My goat. Somebody killed a goat belonging to me.'

'And who put in into your head that this honest man had anything to do with the wicked act? Or myself any more than him? You and your goats with the scour that are living off the neighbours ever and always! Like yourself!'

'You can't trust these fellows,' Murchadh said to me. 'They're likely to lace into each other.'

'Be sure of it, and stay clear of them if they do.'

'All's well, at any rate, so long as 'tis only a battle of words so far.'

'So long as they stick to the words, there's no danger to them.'

But they did not. And it was the owner of the goats that was knocked flat. Some of the men helped to carry him out into the open air. And I fancy nobody would shed a tear over his corpse, if corpse it was. It had been a long time since anyone had used fisticuffs in there. That was another feature of the old way of life, and it dying out.

... At times a word can send a man searching far back in his memory and so it was with me the other night. The word 'sun-child' is what I'm referring to now. I was very young back on the Island when I heard it first, but I did not understand it and I would not rest until I did. There were words in the Catechism and the Ten Commandments that I didn't understand either, and I hardly understand some of them rightly yet, but notice how I never went looking for an explanation of them at all!

It was Maidhc Mhuiris I asked first but he could explain it no more than myself, although he was a year or two older. 'I don't know rightly what it is,' he said, 'but I'll ask when I go home at midday. My father should know, for he knows everything.'

Maidhc went home and came back with the explanation of my word for me. 'Do you know what it is?' he said. 'A baby seal that's left behind on the surface of the sea by the mother while she is diving for a bite to eat for herself.'

'But,' says I to him, 'a baby seal is not a child. Isn't a baby seal a baby seal and no one ever called it a child.'

'I'll ask the schoolmaster so, and he will give me the right answer to the question.'

'Ah, don't. Maybe he mightn't like it.'

'What will we do so? 'Tis the devil altogether if we can't find out what the word means.'

'Never mind,' says I to him. 'There's an old man in the village here who will explain it to me and no bother, old Peaid.'

Peaid was an old man, prying and inquisitive, who knew the ins and outs of everything that ever happened. I strolled in the door to him. He put a question and twenty to me. Was I at school? Where was my father since morning? Had he the winter manuring of the potatoes done yet? Who would be making the lobster pots for him this year? And a long list to tell, so I was beginning to think I would never get a word in. I would have let him carry on firing his questions but I had to go and drive down the cow and calf that had been grazing on the hill since morning. What I did in the finish was to go out the door, saying goodbye to him. Then I turned on my heel again and said, 'Whisper, Peaid, did you ever hear a baby seal called anything else except a baby seal?'

'Wisha, pet, I never heard anything different.'

'You never heard it being called "a sun-child"?'

'Good boy you are!' says he, '"You are better off with meal in your bag instead of chaff," or whoever put such a notion into your little head? That isn't what a baby seal is called, but a child that no father can be found for him. Be off with you now to drive the cow back for yourself and never mind any more questions.'

It was then I understood that there was something strange about the word. If so it did not take long before I figured it out for myself.

Since then I don't suppose I heard the word used by anybody until last night. It was from the woman in Bally-nalackan I heard it, the woman with all the fluency in Gaelic. She was flinging it in the face of one of the neighbours, the woman that drove Bríde from her door on the day of the cocks. I suppose she is the finest speaker of the language in Ireland, blessings on her.

I was rambling round the village taking the air for myself, when I heard the Gaelic flying between the two of them. I had no idea what the cause of the dispute was but, from what I could gather, it was all over a dead hen someone had left in Bríde's garden, and her suspicions fell on the other woman. There are people who would do such a thing and it would not be to bring you luck. Howsoever, Bríde had no proof that the old woman, her neighbour, had done the deed, so what she fell back on was to call her 'a sun-child', the greatest insult she knew to fling at her.

I wonder what it is at all that draws me to Ballynalackan!

... Murchadh has a new cat in the house these days, a big white tom. He has the other cat still, but he is getting old and maybe the fear on Murchadh is of finding the old cat lying stone-dead one fine morning and he would be left on his own then himself. As I have remarked before, he has neither wife nor family and has given up all thought of ever having them.

Be that as it may, he has the new cat now, along with the old one that has been failing for some while, as I have noticed myself. He no longer stayed out by night as much as he used to do, 'And,' says Murchadh, 'anyone that loses interest in these concerns, 'tis all up with him. It is the same case with the animal.'

The new cat is being trained and taught in the same way as the old one. Murchadh would not let the new tenant overstep the mark from the very first day in case he might grow swollen-headed and become too high and mighty. That would never do in Murchadh's house!

While I was there with him today the young cat came in. He looks for all the world like a year-old calf.

Murchadh is a man who pays little heed to Catholic priests or Protestant ministers. 'In their preaching and teaching they are poles apart,' as he puts it. He has no God except the sun and no idols except his two cats and his ass. 'Only for the two of them,' he says, 'where would I be? Isn't it the sun that wakes me up of a morning and sends me to sleep at night? Isn't it the sun that provides me with food and drink and keeps the heat in me? If I want to go to a funeral or to Dingle, isn't it on the fellow in the shed outside that I depend? And isn't it this pair of bastards here under my feet that keep me company day and night? What more do I need?'

The white cat came up to the fire. 'Yeip' is the pet name he has for him; he had no such name for the old one.

The cat moves closer to the fire, wraps his tail round his legs and starts to lick himself. Murchadh eyes him sourly, even though the poor cat has done nothing out of the way. He picks up a stick he keeps beside the hearth and, all unawares, the cat gets a welt of it across the ear that sends him flying on top of his head across the floor.

'Clear off,' says he, 'and the devil go with you! You're back now after your three or four nights out tom-catting, and a thumper of a mouse crunching away beside my head all night long! Clear off, and may God not prosper you! I like my job giving lodgings to the likes of you while you're leaving your seed and your kittens all over the village! May you come to a bad end!'

Murchadh and myself start discussing the affairs of the world again, but before long my white tom saunters back up to us, clean forgetting the trouncing he had received already.

'Look, wisha, Yeip boy,' says Murchadh to him, 'whatever drubbing I give you there is no danger you will ever leave me.'

He rises from his chair and goes down the kitchen to where he keeps the water. He takes out a tin plate on which he has white bread steeping, gets his bottle of milk and pours a splash of it on to the bread. He calls Yeip and the cat runs down to him with his tail in the air, and every mee-ow by him like a child that would be longing for sweets from you.

When Yeip has finished dining he hoists his behind and off out the door he goes from Murchadh. 'Be off now,' he called after him, 'and I hope you're gone for good, if it isn't the almighty hurry you're in to be off! 'Tis how all the cats of the village must be in heat, for you to be in such a hurry out.'

'Whatever would you do without the same cats?' I asked.

'I don't know in the devil. You have a wife to bear the brunt of your teeth and tongue. I can only round on the cat and if we are to face damnation at all, that's what will send me there.'

'You should have brought a little wife into the house for yourself. Faith it isn't too late for you yet.'

'It is not, by my baptism. "No ne'er-do-well but finds a mate to match", and I dare say I could find one still too. My father and mother lived here one time and they with a houseful of us. My father had no work and nothing he could turn his hand to whenever there was a rough sea. He could only be looking at us and he without a bite of food for us. He had to head for Dingle, like a beggarman, to see who would let him have a half sack of flour until things got better.'

'Upon my soul, sure that's how most of us were reared, boy.'

'I know well it was. But tell me this much: how could that kind of hard life give anyone who understood it a mind for marriage? Nobody ever married in a labourer's cottage here except a man that had some touch of madness about him.'

'Isn't it a good thing that the poverty made people turn their backs on all that for a way of life?'

'Faith, it did, when the family saw the trouble and hardship the father had to face. "Hard work teaches hard sense." Anyone who saw the suffering all that produced, only a stepmother would blame him for not letting himself be caught up in it.'

With that we heard the commotion coming from the bedroom at the other end of the house.

'They're there, Murchadh.'

'I know well who is there. 'Tis Yeip, the bastard.'

He went down and what did he find but Yeip and a thumper of a rat in his mouth.

'That's the villain I thought was a mouse last night and be

sure of it, if I knew rightly that's what it was, I would have shifted myself out of there.'

The cat had no great interest in the rat now beyond letting the headman know he had done away with him and this would be a bond of gratitude and friendship between them. He tossed the rat on to the floor, marched himself off out the door again and goodbye to Murchadh.

Murchadh came up and sat in his chair once more. There is poetry and proverb in his Gaelic beyond all the people in Ireland and, if so, he lavished it all on Yeip, praising him to the skies. He heaped such praise on the cat that what Art O'Leary* received wasn't a patch on it. He told about how he brought him home the first day ever, how he would follow him into the bed by night and the racket he made into the late hours with his purring. 'But look,' says he, '"Woe betide the man that fails to give a helping hand to his own in their hour of need."'

'The devil to it, is it all that long since you gave him a good slash of a stick, and if the cat had any sense he would let the rats chew the ears right off you!'

'Ah boy, where would I be if the white cat was a wife and I gave her that belt? Taking a drive with a couple of Guards in an official car, that's where I'd be, and lying on a hard plank bed for a couple of nights. And shamed before the world, to crown it.'

I was just about to pitch Murchadh and his cats to the devil and take myself off when there was a light knock on the door that had been bolted against the wind.

'Go round the back,' he called, 'the door is on the latch.'

---

* Arthur O'Leary was shot by Government troops, in Carriganima, Co. Cork, in 1773 when he refused to sell his famous mare to a Protestant for £5. Under the Penal Laws a Catholic should not possess a horse of greater value; he was bound to hand him over on demand for £5. His wife, Eileen O'Connell, an aunt of Daniel O'Connell, the 'Liberator', composed a famous lament over him.

A child came in straight away by the other door.

'Come hither, little boy,' says Murchadh. 'Is anything the matter with you?'

'No, but the master told me to come and let you know that your white cat is lying dead above beside the schoolhouse. He wants you to go up and take him away from the gable-end.' The child went off out without saying another word.

Murchadh did not speak for a while. 'Maybe with God's help 'tisn't him at all,' he said finally. 'Maybe he isn't my little white cat.'

With that I happened to glance out the window and what did I see but a couple of older schoolboys carrying a sack with something in it. They left the sack and its contents outside Murchadh's door and made off. I didn't think Murchadh had noticed them at all, and I supposed it was the white cat in the sack. When they had gone I told him about the two boys leaving the sack and out he went. He saw it, picked it up and let the white cat roll out of it on to the ground. His head was crushed like the head of a fledgling bird that had been dropped from the claws of a hawk.

'God help us,' he said and he said no more for a while, as if a son or daughter was dead. 'God help us and Mary his mother,' he said then. 'Isn't it the sudden death to be run over, and isn't the person walking along the roads greatly to be pitied?'

I had pity for himself, the poor man, in one way, though he was not to be pitied in another. 'You have another cat, Murchadh.'

'I have and I haven't. He's an old cat and has not long more to live.'

'Even so, before long more the offspring of the white cat will be all over the village. Won't there be a kitten to be had in some quarter?'

'There will, I suppose, whoever lives to see it.'

'There's a lesson to be learnt by you from your cat, Murchadh.'

'How is that?'

'If the cat was like yourself and stayed clear of the females, wouldn't you be left without his offspring tomorrow or the day after? And if those able to give you a helping hand bestirred themselves as little and were as sour as yourself, what would you do in your hour of need? That's not how the white cat behaved. And if he got his due he would have a cats' funeral procession from here to Cathair Deargáin, the likes of which has never been seen in Corcaguiny.'

I left him speechless. Maybe I was too hard on him.

. . . An easterly wind and a calm sea is what we have at present. A man might judge it good weather for the trawl-line, and he would not be far wrong. The Captain is a man who possesses every kind of fishing gear. Nets, a boat, trawl-lines, he has them all, and himself as fine a skipper as any ever in Newfoundland.

Leaning against a fence-wall I was, gazing out to sea, when he came along after digging a handful of potatoes for himself. 'I was thinking,' says he, telling me what was in his mind, 'that instead of being in here we would be better off making a run out and we would have the bait for the trawl-line.'

'I'm your man,' I told him, 'if you had two more,' and I knowing full well that he only had to beckon to Bod and Com and they would come running.

'Oh, have no fear about them joining you,' he said. I didn't need him to tell me that!

We had not been out together again since the night of the great sea-animal. I went off home and put the case before the 'Queen'. 'Whisper now, boy,' she said, 'is it how you have some notion in your head of getting mixed up with those devils again? And here I would be pacing the floor for two days, counting the cross-beams as I wait for you to come back, and that not certain. On top of it you're going out with those good-for-nothings.'

I let her have her head for I knew she would quieten down of her own accord. She always does so long as I don't answer her back. I drank a mouthful of tea for myself and made a bundle of my things and a few cuts of bread. I was on my way out the door when she shouted to me to come back. I came back in again and got a big splash of holy water between the two eyes from her. 'Go now and may the devil not go the road with you!' was what she said to me.

I headed northwards and, judging from the preparations made already, there could be no doubt but my pair of dog-fishes had been in the village since midday. Hadn't they the best excuse in the world! They were bursting for action, and the eagerness of one was a spur to the other.

The boat was ready and everything on board. 'God knows, they have been stoking up properly,' I said to myself, 'and they to be all set to go out without paying the usual visit to the "Well".'

We put to sea with the Captain aft at the helm and no word out of anybody. It would have been wasted anyway with the noise coming from the engine behind. When I looked back at my Captain I said to myself that this boat was a far cry from Dáire Donn's canoe.* We left Smerwick Harbour behind and steamed west past the Submerged Rocks out towards Tiaracht. When we came in sight of the lighthouse we slackened speed and cast the nets, leaving them moored for over an hour.

---

* A reference to Fenian legend. It was believed that Dáire Donn, King of the World, was defeated by the roving warrior-band, the Fianna, at the Battle of Ventry, near the Great Blasket Island. It lasted a year and a day.

'Start hauling in to me,' Com said to Bod, 'the man aft is fast asleep and the three of us will haul them in ourselves. If we can't, I'll call himself.'

Bod passed the rope to him and we caught hold of a corner of the net. There were two mackerel dangling in it. A couple more fathoms were brought in and we saw nine or ten fish still alive. 'Let them go for now,' said Bod, 'maybe 'tis rising the fish are.'

We paid out the rope and lowered the nets again. Before long we heard the coughing and heaving about from the stern of the boat. The Captain had woken up and with no idea of his bearings at first. When he read the compass he let out a roar.

'Haul in those nets so that we can be making for home to bait the trawl-line.'

We hauled in once more, finding no fish in the inner nets, but as we had more nets to come we ended up with plenty of bait for the trawl-line.

The engine was started up and we made neither stop nor stay until her stem touched Ballydavid Quay once again. Every man was doing the work of two from now on, baiting the hooks and cutting bait as hard as he could. We were half-way through when Bod complained that there was a thirst on him and boiling heat for lack of a drop to drink; his head was spinning from cutting the mackerel and if he had one half glass itself it would make a man of him.

'I'm not feeling too well myself from the work,' Com put it.

'Whisper now, ye two sons of bitches,' said the Captain, 'is it a humour for fishing that's on ye, or for boozing? Give over yeer capers now and put yeer shoulders to the wheel in earnest! The trawl-lines will have to be shot an hour before daybreak, but from the way ye're going about it . . .!' and he let fly a couple of curses that made the pair of them hop.

They shook themselves up and they having to be satisfied

with the drop gone cold in the pit of their bellies by now. But they had a notion, I fancy, that the Captain would have some bottle aboard, and Bod had hit upon a shift to come by it.

We stowed everything away in proper order and put out to sea once more. There was no great humour on some of us, it seemed, and no one would have much to say till morning unless relief came from some quarter.

We made the sign of the Cross for the journey and for the day and whatever hardship lay ahead of us. We were well out with a breath of east wind there, and Mount Brandon coming partly into view, as we took our bearings from the first buoy we had dropped. We shot the trawl-lines, each man of us doing the work of two with fervour and zeal.

We had a couple of hours' delay now, longer maybe, waiting for daylight. You must wait for day to brighten before you can haul in. As we had time on our hands Bod put his head under his wing and in no time there was every snore coming from him. When Com saw him fast asleep he arranged a bundle of rags for his own head and stretched back on the thwart. Soon his mouth was sagging open.

The Captain was aft and I went back to him, for I had no wish for sleep myself. He pulled out the bottle. 'Here you are,' says he, 'before that pair forward notice a thing. If they knew it was here they wouldn't do a stroke for me until they had it drained. But leave a drop in the bottom for fear there might be a call for it.'

I took a swig and I in need of it after the night. There is no time worse for a man when he is out on the sea than waiting for dawn to break.

'Glory be to God,' cried the Captain, 'what's that heading towards me?'

It was like a big city sailing all lit up on the water.

'She's making straight for us, boy,' says I.

'If she is, and at the speed she's going, 'tis how she'll sink us if she comes any closer. I'll call Bod and Com.'

'Never mind Bod and Com,' said I. 'When she draws near she will wake those two, you can be sure. And won't you have it to boast that 'tis at the bottom of the sea they would have been only for yourself being the skipper? And they would rather have a bundle of blazing straw stuck under their arses than that.'

The words were hardly out of my mouth when the floating city had drawn alongside. The first question her captain put to us was what kind of fishing were we doing. We told him it was trawl-lines but that we had none of them hauled in yet. At this point Bod started up from his sleep and saw the city looming overhead.

'Keep out you bastard!' he shouted up in English.

He had got into a bit of a panic when he saw all the lights blazing above him. But 'pon my soul, my man above knocked a start out of him when he called back in Irish: 'Let ye have no fear, ye're in no danger.' It was then we realized what vessel it was—the *Macha*.* The captain said they would be at anchor in Smerwick Harbour until four in the evening and, if we had any catch, to bring it to him on our way home. He said goodbye and sailed away.

It was then we thought of the buoy of our trawl-lines. The big vessel had put it clean out of our heads; we found that she had sunk it. The night was pitch black still and it difficult to see anything in the water. Patience and endurance were called for now, and these are what a man at sea must have. Bod was the first to sight it in the distance. 'I can see something on the water over there to the east, though it could be a sea-bird,' he said. He was right. There was something. Bod took the wheel himself and came up to the buoy. 'There it is for ye now,' he

---

* Irish Government patrol vessel.

said, 'and the man is to be pitied that would put ye steering a boat. Anyone depending on ye is lost.'

It was Bod who had something to brag about after all, and not the Captain.

We hauled in and there were two fine big eels on the nearest hooks. Some people would rather have eel than a pig's head. We caught pollock, cod, ling, ray big and small. We had more eels too. We caught a huge fine fat halibut that was six feet long. And soon we were hauling in a tope that was all tangled up in the trawl-line and was gashed and torn by it. With the second trawl-line we drew in a huge ray along with another big fish that was the length of the boat.

The sun was sending out its beams and we tackling the third line. We had two crawfish along with many more fish of all sizes. As soon as the Captain saw the crawfish he jumped for joy, saying that whoever lived to see the coming summer would find this a good place for setting lobster pots.

Says Com: 'Today we're up ploughing with the lark, tomorrow we can sleep till it's dark.'

We were hauling away fine when suddenly the Captain gave a shout: 'O Christ, the barb of the hook has gone into my finger!'

Com darted back and put his knife to the snood, leaving the end of it dangling from the hook stuck in the Captain's hand. Bod dashed back then and slipped the knife between the flesh of the hand and the hook. He got the hook free saying, 'There you are now, if you have any drop in your bladder let it fall on the cut.' The Captain did as he was told, an old rag was tied round his finger and so it was left.

Before we had the last trawl-line hauled in we became aware of a mist coming on, a heat haze I suppose, but all kinds of mist are the same to you when you are out on the sea. We stayed where we were for an hour but the mist was showing no sign of ever lifting and it high tide by this time. Our fear now was that it would not lift before ebb-tide, especially if it was a heavy mist at all.

I thought I heard a fog-horn landwards. The others heard it too. It put great heart in us to know there were others out in the mist besides ourselves. She was heading in our direction and when we were sure of her position we started up the engine and steered towards her. She was between us and land and had sighted us before we saw her.

That was when our spirits rose. Mist cannot be called bad weather but all the same, when you have been caught out in it for any length of time, all kinds of changes are in store for you. You have no wish for chat or whiling away the time. Every hour feels as long as three. Even if someone is making conversation you find no satisfaction in what he has to say, for the mist is coming between you. There is no work or activity going on, only your two eyes straining to see if you can catch a glimpse of land or sun or moon.

We drew alongside the vessel. She was the *Macha*. She had an idea, I suppose, that we were caught in the mist. A couple of rubber fenders were lowered so that our boat would not scrape the paint off her. The men above had come to the gunwhale and there was every whoop out of them over all the fish in our boat. Baskets were lowered and two lads came down with them. They picked out the fish they wanted and up they were hoisted, baskets and lads together. Grand mugs of tea were lowered to us then and cuts of white bread buttered on both sides. There was a welcome for them, I promise you.

A bottle of brandy was lowered by way of payment. The captain of the *Macha* shouted down that he preferred the two fresh crawfish to all the brandy he had on board. 'And now,' says he, 'I'll take ye in on tow if that suits ye.'

'It does, by my baptism,' our own Captain replied.

Everything was made ready and away with us through the surf behind the *Macha*. We knocked back a couple of slugs of the brandy and from then on no one would think to look at us that we had any poor relations. When the drop of brandy went coursing through the blood of the other three, their faces lit up and they were not looking like death any more. I felt a new man myself along with them. Com claimed and Bod claimed, and the Captain argued against the pair of them, that it was himself who had brought the rest of us safe out of the mist. Each of the three of them was trying to shout the others down with his boasting. Without any doubt it was easy to set them off after the night they had been through, and they having nothing in their bellies since the night before.

We said goodbye to the *Macha* when she released the tow-rope and in no time we had drawn in at the Quay. The boat was moored, the fish were cleaned, the trawl-lines stowed away and the boat was left at anchor, secured for a full year and a day.

'Go along, Com,' said the Captain to him, 'and find some means of carrying these fish to market.'

Com rode off on his bicycle, and he as fresh after the night as the parish priest setting out to say Mass for the congregation.

After half an hour or so, and we having everything ready now, a tractor came along but the driver had no news of Com, nor had anyone else.

'No news is good news,' says Bod. 'But rest assured, that fellow knows which side his bread is buttered.'

When the man in the tractor had taken the fish away we were clearing up and putting things in proper order and, as bad luck would have it, what should come along but two big motors and one of them had a bicycle in the boot. They drew up and a man stepped out asking us where our fish had gone. We told him and with that he opened the rear door of the car and lifted our man out dead to the world, laying him down carefully on the ground. He hauled the bicycle out and left it leaning against the fence. Then he turned his car round and off they all drove after the fish.

Bod walks over to Com to see how he is. He kneels down to listen to his heart and after a while, like an expert keener, he raises a fine, steady lament over the corpse that rouses up the neighbourhood. Along came women and children, and the district nurse was sent for. She said there was breath in him still and that somebody should go for the priest and the doctor; he was not beyond hope yet.

At that point the two motors came back. A man jumped out and took a look at Com. He pulled out his watch, saying it would be another half-hour before he woke out of the deep sleep he was in. He was a doctor himself, he told us, and there was nothing the matter with Com except that he had drunk too much brandy after fasting too long.

They were English people that Com happened to meet on the Ballynalackan road. They were heading for Ballyferriter and gave him a lift. They all had a good drop taken before they made for Ballydavid.

''Twas well I knew,' said Bod, 'as I said before, that my Com knows which side his bread is buttered.'

We went into the public house for a while with the English people. They stood to us generously and freely; soon the tiredness of the day and the night had lifted and we were as lively as a tune on the fiddle.

Bod took hold of the melodeon and started playing away like the dickens so that you'd swear to look at him it was a Sunday afternoon after Mass.

'What about the man lying outside?' asked the Captain.

'If it was you or me,' said Bod, 'lying out there where he is, and he was where we are, what do you imagine he would be doing? I'll tell you, his mouth would be wide open and he'd be laughing his head off. God of bright glory, 'tis little you know of Com's trickery, my poor Captain!'

While Bod was playing away the Englishmen, and the women with them, started prancing about in some kind of a dance to Bod's music, music they were unaccustomed to, not that it bothered them. Bod wasn't bothered either and there was never king or knight as pleased as he was, playing away for them and they straining to keep up with him. Only a stepmother would blame him for it.

'On my soul, Bod,' I said, 'we're in a place now where we won't be caught in any mist and no fog-horn will need to be sounded for us.'

'Yerra, man, isn't it God, praise be to him for ever, that sends the rough and the smooth to us, and isn't yesterday's sorrow today's solace? I wouldn't be in such high spirits playing this melodeon only for what happened to us this morning.'

'Wisha, God rest your soul, Com!' says I, 'if you were alive now isn't it up to your ears the froth of the porter would be?'

'God help us!' he said, 'isn't a man carried off quickly after all, or whatever did for him?'

With that, Bod pricked up his ears. I also had heard the sound outside.

'I hear the corncrake calling,' he said, 'and I do not like it, for the corncrake settled down to sleep for herself a good while ago, and 'tis unnatural for her to be abroad at this time of the year. Isn't the hay stacked for the past two months, so where could the corncrake come from?'

The words were hardly out of his mouth when in our man came, and he looking as fresh as at any time in his life. The doctor from England handed him a drink.

'Upon my soul,' declared Bod, 'that will clear the worms out of people that are in sore need of it, and the gap in the fence there for them to sleep it off again with the help of God.'

Com turned to the Englishman declaring that poor Bod was not in his right mind and no notice should be taken of him, for it was high time he was confined to the madhouse.

'I'd give anything,' says the doctor, 'to be as healthy as you are in every way.'

'You must be in a poor way so, wisha,' says Bod, 'for there isn't one of us but is fit to be put away in the madhouse and left there. And if we are, let it be for keeps!'

'That isn't a nice thing for you to say in front of ladies and gentlemen,' said Com.

'I could easily tell, as I said before, that no good would come from the call of the corncrake, and see how right I was.'

'I'm thinking,' says the Captain, 'that 'tis time for all of ye to be gathering yeerselves off home. 'Tis time for ye ever since the middle of yesterday.'

We trudged home tired to the world and we not sure whether it was the hardship or the carousing that had played the devil with us more. The 'Queen' was waiting for me with black looks, but she was aware that we were safe and sound ashore since morning.

'You did it again!' she said. 'You did, boy. It isn't the first time, nor the second, nor the third by you. Soon you will be the sole talk of the village. But that was ever the way with you. Let you have your own way always, give you your head and you're laughing . . .'

I had no great wish to argue with her for I was weary and worn out and I offered up her words as a penance. I ate my bite and went to sleep for myself.

It was morning when I woke up and, 'pon my soul, the sleep

had made a new man of me. I took a stroll outside and the beautiful weather would bring joy to anyone, weather such as we seldom see at this time of the year. It was a Saturday and there is something about a Saturday that makes it different from every other day in the week. It brings an air of restfulness with it and nobody is inclined to do very much because you have Sunday following on. It is our custom always to shave on the Saturday and that marks the end of work and business—any day you have shaved!

There were one or two small items left unfinished from the night before, the trawl-lines to be put in order and suchlike, so I decided to make my way northwards. I filled my pipe and reddened it. I took the port road, the short cut up. I was feeling fresh as a river eel, and the hardship all forgotten.

When I drew near the landing place there wasn't a Christian to be seen. I looked east and west, and then I saw the legs of the man under a currach. Who was it but Bod with his head resting on the thwart.*

'Who have we here?' I asked.

'It's me,' answered Bod promptly.

'Have you any news of the other pair?'

'The Captain is east in the sheds. I suppose 'tis waiting for us he is.'

'And what about Com? Or is it dead he is?'

'There's a danger of him! Sure if that fellow was dead wouldn't the news of it be broadcast on the wireless? He's dead all right, boy!'

'It isn't the heat that sent you looking for shade?'

'Indeed it isn't the heat but the scalding thirst that drove me here and I'd rather not meet anyone for a week unless I get a cure.'

---

* On shore the currachs were laid upside-down on stanchions.

'Let's be making our way east to the Captain. We'll have to finish off what's left to do at any rate.'

We headed east and when we looked inside the sheds we found the Captain sitting on a stool gazing out to sea.

'For God's sake, what's up with you, you poor man?'

'Ye'll see straight away when ye come to settle up,' he answered.

'Have you any notion what fish fetched yesterday?' Bod asked.

'It would be no wonder if it fetched fifty pounds,' he said.

'If so, and you were paid that much, be thankful,' said Bod.

Teasing him the Captain was of course, for he knew well what price it made.

'It fetched, wisha boy, as much as sixty pounds and I never expected it to reach half that.'

'You could easily know from those fish that they would make a high price. They were worth calling fish. If you had them in the Dublin market last night they would have reached a hundred and fifty pounds,' I said myself.

With that who should come along from the west but Com.

'Now then, come on and we'll put these trawl-lines in some kind of order,' he said.

'We may as well hang them up, wisha,' I agreed. The Captain said nothing; he only followed us.

We went to the shed where we had stowed the trawl-lines away, and what should we find but a dog hanging out of the window with a hook stuck in his mouth, and he in a frenzy. We took no great notice of the dog's plight, for it wasn't the first time such a thing had happened. Com took out his knife and cut the snood; he let the dog run off with the hook still in him.

'"The man that owns the cow must go under her tail," ' says Bod. 'Let the man that owns the dog pull the hook out since he didn't stay out of mischief.'

Midday

We lifted the latch on the door, only to find four big tomcats inside with most of the trawl-lines tangled round them. Each of them had a hook in his mouth and he looking as cross as the devil. Only a brave man would venture near to straighten things out. But all Com wants is chances like this so that he can be showing off, and of course Bod has him sized up and is the right man to drive him to the limit.

'They'll stay there,' declared Bod. 'Dread wouldn't let me tackle them. I have poor courage, Seán,' he said, looking straight at me and pinching me on the thigh at the same time. 'You'd have to have great courage to go near them.'

''Tis the same with myself, wisha,' I said.

We knew this was all Com needed. He had only to hear that we were frightened and he would thrust himself into the fires of hell. And he did! He set about cats, hooks, and trawl-lines and, before he was finished, hooks were sticking to the tie-beams, cats were up on the loft, and the trawl-lines were all over the place. He caught hold of the first cat, drew his knife on the snood and sent him flying out the door with a kick.

'There's great breeding in him,' said Bod, puffing him up. 'Is there any of the Island breeding in him, Seán?'

'There could be, 'pon my soul.'

That was enough to make Com feel really proud; another cat was set free and sent off with the hook stuck in him. Com was delighted entirely that the cats had us quivering with dread. He had two cats to free still that had a whole trawl-line twisted round them. After the devil's own struggle with one of them, he managed to get hold of the snood and give it the knife. The cat shot out the door with pepper under his tail. A whoop came from Bod and before he drew breath the second cat was on his way out.

'My life on you!' cried Bod. 'There's no holding the man of courage.'

It was then Com tumbled to it that the other fellow had been leading him on.

'On my soul,' he said, 'but ye're the fine pair of tricksters, the two of ye! And it would be hard to catch ye sticking yeer necks out, but I'm not quite the fool ye take me for.'

'It's as well for us to hurry on and hang the trawl-lines up straight away,' I put in, for fear it might come to blows between them.

When we were finished the Captain called us to share out our pennies and a good night's pay it was. We went into the public house, the goat was skinned and put roasting. But when my own thoughts went back to the 'Queen' and the day before, I made the sign of the Cross, for it was well I knew the others would catch it hot and strong that evening.

Evening

Evening

❦

Such are the people, some of them at any rate, and such is
the life around us here. Some of us are better than others and
some are worse. But aren't we all the better for sharing our
lives together, as they say?

It did not take me long at all, or the 'Queen' either, to settle
down after coming out from the Island. The people we met
here were no different from those we left behind in the other
place. The only thing was that the paths we had trodden in our
youth were over there and it wasn't easy to put those out of our
thoughts. We came to know new neighbours and they came to
know us. They are honest folk, straight as a die.

But, as my uncle told me the day after I came, 'As you treat
them, so will they treat you.' I never forgot his advice and that
same uncle raised me a step in their eyes when the news spread
that I was his sister's son. I had been there only one day when I
came across a couple of men who invited me to go fishing with
them. I went along in all innocence, but appearances are
deceptive. A new currach had been built for these two and they
had promised a place in it to the son of a poor man who had no
experience and had never even been to sea before. But they
hoped to persuade me to join them and that, since I was a
stranger, I would take no interest in the ins and outs of it.

I had been going out fishing with them for over a week and
they never mentioned a word about the new currach. But when
there is jiggery-pokery going on, the undercurrents from it
come to the surface, and so it was with my pair. It is a habit

131

with fishermen to go for a drink on Sunday evenings. A man from the west of the parish would meet a man from the east and often sell a net and oars; an assortment of other articles too, all dirt cheap, for everyone who could manage it came looking for the bargain.

With this in mind I strolled north on the Sunday evening. Beside the fence on the way up from the harbour there was a big wooden plank on which fishermen used to sit chatting about this and that.

When I looked towards the plank it was packed with men, for all the world like a flock of cormorants on the Beannach* on a scorching summer's day. I greeted them and they replied politely and civilly. A man stood up and invited me to take his place; he had been sitting there for some while now, he said, and was thinking of 'going on the udder'. I was a while pondering over what he had said before I realized what he meant. I thought at first he was intending to go and milk the cows! But I was not long in the dark.

They were making me dizzy with questions about the Island, although there were few of them that did not know the place and especially the sea around it. Many of these men used to go fishing in Dingle Bay years before and had come to know the sea around the Island well.

The man who had stood up asked me if I'd like to join him 'on the udder', and I wouldn't say no to him in front of the company. We went into the public house and I was no sooner inside the door than he drew down my two partners to me and the new currach, explaining the whole case from start to finish, though he gave me no advice about what to do. That man has gone to his eternal reward now.

My two partners suited me fine, but what was I to do in this situation? They had promised the young lad a berth in the new

* A rock on one of the small islands off the Great Blasket.

currach as soon as it was ready to take out. 'But,' says I to myself, 'what would I have done if I had never met them?' I had a sound enough currach of my own if I could find the right partner. But that was no easy matter amongst fishermen, when every likely man has already secured a berth for himself. That is one fear haunting the fisherman every day and hour of his life.

Monday came, the start of a new week with everybody going about his work. I headed north along the main road and then turned down towards the harbour. I sat myself down on the plank, filled my pipe and lit it. I gazed east and I gazed west, taking in all that was going on and soon now I would have a clear picture of the place in my mind.

I hadn't quite finished the pipe when my pair came along. To give them their due, they did not hide their heads like men trying to give you the slip. The exact opposite was what they had in mind. They were coming straight to see me and put the case before me in full. They told me the story, how they had fixed up with this young lad to become one of the crew, but if I came along as a fourth man they would be more than satisfied with that for an arrangement.

I discussed the case in full with them both, explaining my own position, and by the time I had finished I was a little tin god in their eyes. We parted for the time being and, far from any disagreement between us, there was the opposite entirely. They were most interested in my promise that they could call on me again if things didn't work out, and the sea and the fishing did not suit the young lad. They were in high fettle going off to fetch and launch the new currach, and they giving the lad his chance, make or break.

There were old men around here in those days who were drawing the pension, and when the pension book is handed to you your fishing days are over and will never return. This is not from feebleness or failing health but, when a fisherman who has spent his life at sea is handed this book, he has no choice except to join the *jainglérí* for a while, be it long or short, according to God's will. *Jainglérí* spend one night at sea and the next ashore, and if they have no catch after two good casts of the net, they prefer to head for home rather than stay out fishing.

The story spread, once the new currach was afloat, that the Islandman was in search of a crew. I wasn't kept waiting long at all. Along came a hardy, strong, solid block of an old man; he wasn't all that nimble, this was the only thing.

'Whisper, my good man,' he said to me, 'have you any crew tonight?'

'No,' I told him. 'Have you any old net at all?'

'Yes, I have, two of them. And Micil my partner above here has two more. And from my reading of the weather it will make a great night for *jainglérí*.

'Come along the pair of ye, boy,' I said to him. 'I'd rather see ye bringing something in for yeerselves than to be as ye are.' Sure God help us all, these were no two old codgers, but men who knew their trade.

The mackerel season had not started properly yet, but they had made their appearance early, for that was a glorious summer altogether and when the sea remains settled the fish start shoaling on the surface, as they were doing now. It was this that caused the fishermen to settle with one another early. I was in the boat of the *jainglérí* now and I having that title too. Both men suited me, for the age was the only difference I saw between them, and if age and experience are needed anywhere it is on the sea.

The week passed and the *jainglérí* had their pay at the end of it as well as the men in their prime, and if it was no more than some had, neither was it any less. We spent another week slogging away, but 'it isn't every day Dónall Buí is marrying' and the fish became harder to find. It was not the fishing season proper, only mackerel shoaling, and fish like that are no sooner there than they have disappeared again. We had spent a couple of nights out without catching a thing and when the old men saw the fish failing, they began to wilt themselves. They said they would rather be drawing home a sod of turf for themselves for the winter, than be travelling the cold sea. Nothing suited me better, for I had my own jobs to do around the cabin.

My currach was hauled up on to its stand and I brought my nets home. They were in need of tanning and mending, because I would have to have them in good trim when the fishing season proper came, if I was spared. With all that I had to do around the house it was how I was in no hurry for it to start. But others were in a different case and they were all ready to go.

We found it hard to manage when we came here first without hen or cock, duck or goose. We had no cow, calf, or ass—the fowl and the animals we yearned after, and it was a hardship to manage without them. It was often the talk between us would come to a stop when we saw a cow or an ass passing along, and it was often I saw the tears flowing from the 'Queen's' eyes when this happened.

It came as no surprise to me, for it was herself mostly that used to look after them, the cow being her special care, and I fancy that parting from the cow grieved her even more than leaving the Island. But, sure, there were many things we had to leave behind and it was the last we would ever see of them. That was not the case with ourselves alone, it was the same with every Islander.

Howsoever, time smoothes away the great scars life leaves on a man. The mark of sorrow was on us but it was nothing to feel shame over, it only did us credit, for it was for loss of our native place the sorrow was on us.

Married men were drawing a small allowance from the Government at this period and only for that it is my belief few poor men would be married in the place. That same allowance was the greatest boon that ever came to us from the Government and, without it, many a family man would have had to take himself off across the sea. So, there are people and their families who would not be here at all today without this assistance and it is many the good prayer mothers of children have offered up for the man that brought it in.

Here we had to get along like everyone else and when we needed help from a neighbour—as we did often—it was there for us with a welcome. We obtained an ass and cart, the same as everyone else around possessed , for without them you could neither sow nor reap, nor could you travel far from home to fetch anything. I found the cart strange at first for I had little experience of anything like it. We hadn't one on the Island, no more than anyone else. And, as the man from the Island said long ago, when a Dunquin man offered him a lift to Clochar in his ass and cart, 'God forbid, wisha, I'd much rather walk there, for fear it would make me sea-sick!'

I did know something about it all the same, for I had seen one before and given it a trial.

We had the ass and cart now; we were every bit as good as the neighbours and feeling no envy of them any more.

But my woe and for my sins! We had neither field nor pasture for the ass and could only let him graze along the roadside. To be sure there were others in the same plight as ourselves, but we were strangers in the place and would not like to have our animal caught trespassing.

This sent our thoughts back to the Island again, where we had full and plenty for ass and cow; now the rabbits from the sandhills had the run of the place. But what good was it thinking of the past? That day was gone and it would never return. Still and all, it was no easy matter for us to put the thought of it out of our minds, far from it. It needed the passage of time, the only healer for every disease that has no other cure.

When a fine day would come, one of us would say to the other: 'Dear God, isn't this a grand day they have on the Island?' Whichever one of us said it would wish it back, for it brought no pleasure, the opposite only.

'Why didn't you stay when you were there?' the other would retort. 'What's to stop you going back and staying there till the seagulls pluck the eyes out of you? Isn't it many a person went to America and came home again inside a year? Now is the time for you to go back to the Island again. I am perfectly willing, whatever is in store for us there.'

That is how we would be on at each other when there was nobody present but our two selves. But when the bad day and bad weather came, it was a different story entirely, 'On my soul,' one of us would say, 'the mainland is the place to be today, far from the north west wind battering at us from Yellow Island and Banc an Bhóidí, lashing the waves up into the air; far too from the foam of the breakers at Cliff Mouth while you watch your chance to see if you can force your way through them to go into Limbo.'

That would change the tune!

Our child had reached school age and there was a Government grant available for every child you had at school who spoke Irish, except the first one. As we had only the one we were not eligible, and so were the butt of endless gibes over why we were not finding another child on the strand, and so forth. Sure, it was how we were searching as hard as we could unknown to them!

Evening

Seldom a day passed without my uncle paying us a visit and, from the moment he came in the door until he left, mackerel and lobsters and fishing generally were all he talked about with us. And well he might, for he was a man who knew that trade. All the neighbours used to be in and out too, most of them weighing us up to give themselves something to gossip about when they got back home. But their like are to be found on the Island as well as here for, wherever you find yourself, there will be people watching your every move. Sure how would any of us survive without food for gossip and we idle? They meant us no harm, as they proved in our hour of trial and trouble. They were like the neighbours we had known before.

When the child started school, and was coming and going with the children of the village, it was some ease to us. It helped us to forget and we were settling in amongst our new neighbours. When you have a young child growing up, you try to do your best for her if you can. So, when we saw she was in safe keeping now on the mainland, it put the Island in the sea out of our heads, for we were aware we would be staying here for the sake of the child and that we were finished with the Island for good and all. Of course, it did not make us forget entirely and, to this day, our thoughts fly back, and no living Christian there at all now. As I have said before, isn't it there the roads and paths of our youth are, and they will stay in our minds until we are laid under the clay. You never forget your native place.

So long as a man has the health he must not complain, even if it is health without wealth itself. I never knew a day when I had to complain about my health and, but for that, I'm sure I could not have pulled along as well as I did in a strange place. I knew in my own mind early on that the Island's days were numbered; it was like a vessel sinking and down it would go to the bottom. We used to go back on a visit during the summer, for the 'Queen's' people were still there, her father and mother and her three brothers. We would take the child in with us and, on that account, herself did not like to stay too long on the Blasket; two nights or three at the most.

When we returned after these visits our fondness for the place here grew stronger than ever. We had become aware of the solitude and eeriness hanging over the rock in comparison with the place outside. Clamour and noise outside, the quiet of the dead inside, even though people were living there still, people too who would rather be there than in Paradise. Of course they had not tasted the pastures outside yet.

But, my sorrow! A lingering disease tells its own tale and, however long the day, the night must surely follow. Night came down on the Island too after all the signs that had been making themselves plain for long enough.* This put an end to regret and sorrow, for the source of our sorrow no longer remained.

'Live now, or die where you are,' said the 'Queen' to me. 'The place that was all in all to you is gone from you.'

It was true for her, for a place without people is no place. All we could do from now on was give our minds properly to the place where we were and accept it for what it was; we had to give up our yearning entirely.

Well, the fishing started again, and there is nothing like work for scattering useless thoughts. A man is better off with a hundred mackerel than with foolishness. The stack had been well set up in the haggard by now and this is the very sign people around here go by that the autumn fishing season has begun. The shoaling fish had sunk and any time now would be rising to swim nearer the surface until Christmas, given the right weather.

A hundred mackerel fetched good money in those days with

* The Great Blasket was evacuated in 1953.

men eagerly waiting to catch them at every hour of the night, and they in constant danger of losing their lives. Long years had passed during which there had been no market for mackerel, but the Second World War was raging now and all kinds of fish were snapped up at high prices, even the dogfish. There are folk in this world, fishermen for the most part, and it is little notice they take of putting their very lives at risk, so long as they think money can be made. This must be put down to lack of sense and understanding, but if sense is backed by mature judgement, see what it can do.

The *jaingléirí* and myself joined forces and I would not rather have the Prime Minister and his Deputy along with me, nor would they have been better help. I knew it was neither from greed nor a desire for worldly wealth that they were going out fishing, but simply to have the price of the pint and the plug of tobacco; the fish never left them short of these. As one of them said to me ''Tis how you have livened us up too much, O'Crohan!'

'Ye're not taking a shred of my share from me,' I told him, ''tis yeer own fair honest share ye're taking for yeerselves. Ye don't owe me any thanks at all.'

The next night when we had just cast the nets my Diarmaid, one of the pair, hauls his two fishing lines towards him. He puts a piece of mackerel as bait on a hook and he hasn't the line properly in the water before a fish starts tugging it out of his hand.

''Pon my soul, boy, they're there!' he said and he hauls in a thumper of a hake weighing twelve pounds at the least.

The other man was at the prow and before I knew what was happening he had another on board himself.

'Lamb of God!' says I to myself, 'What kind of men are these at all or where did they pick up the know-how and the skill for fishing?'

Evening

'You have no hook or line, Jack?' says Peaid to me.

'I haven't, nor have I any great use for one, because we never took a line along when we went out with nets.'

'Don't be without,' he said, throwing a spare line to me and a hook with bait on it the likes of which I had never seen. The hook was a foot and a half long with up to three inches of mackerel bait stuck on it.

'Take note of the bait you have on it now,' says he, 'and every bait you put on should be as big.'

'I know as little about how to tackle this, Peaid, as if I came from Márthain.'*

'Upon my soul,' said Peaid, 'if it was from Márthain you came you would know your trade, for 'tis little those rogues don't know.'

My two partners were hauling in hake galore now. I had not cast my line yet nor had I any great wish to do so for fear I would catch no hake at all. I would be the *jaingléir* then! I made the sign of the Cross and lowered my line and hook. Peaid told me the fish were sixteen or seventeen fathoms down and to take soundings accordingly. I let the line drop and when it had gone down the depth I was told I tugged at it, and as soon as I did the fish tugged harder.

'A godsend!' said I under my breath, 'I have a nibble at any rate.'

It did not take me long to haul my hake on board, and a 12-year-old boy would not have been as proud of the deed as I was. Out I threw the line again and straight away I was hauling in, with another hake caught. Peaid spoke from the prow. ''Tis no mushroom growth you are, Jack, and you make no great boast of what you can do. Márthain a while ago, and craftsman now!'

* Hill and district inland.

141

Evening

Each of us was hauling them in, one after another, for a good while, but the *jaingléirí* were growing jaded, for you have to be able to use your limbs when dealing with a hake while he is on the hook; he has only to give the one spin to break free. My two partners were masters of their craft and by the time we were finished with the hake our catch was so big that what mackerel we were netting seemed of little account. We hauled in the nets before time and headed for home with a boat laden with fish, mackerel and hake.

In this way one year went by and two years. We never noticed them passing, what with fishing and earning money and working, with no stop from Monday to Saturday, winter and summer. I came in from the sea one day, not expecting anything, when the 'Queen' told me she wasn't feeling too well. I had been anxious about her for some time, and with good grounds, because the labour pains would be bound to start sooner or later. I rushed off and fetched the doctor and midwife. Within a couple of hours another daughter was born to me and all was safe.

This brought a great change around the hearth from then on. When the time for the baptism came I was asked what I would like the child to be christened, and faith I had the name ready, one I preferred to any other name under the sun. I had an aunt in the village called Cáit and her name above any in Ireland would be a credit to the child. And I had a sister called Cáit, the sister who got into difficulties while bathing with Eibhlín Nicholls off the White Strand of the Island. My brother Dónall and Eibhlín saved her, though both of them were drowned in the attempt.*

* Eibhlín Nicholls, a visitor to the Island, became friends with Cáit. Dónall, 18 years old and a good swimmer, was digging potatoes near his house when he saw the girls in difficulties; he ran to help.

Evening

I told the 'Queen' my reasons for wanting this name and she was quite happy with it. It was just as well, for I was not going to suggest any other. Niamh was the name of our first child and the mother was asked to call her this even before she was born. A girl from Dublin, Niamh Fitzgerald,* used to spend the summer on the Blasket and our first child was named after her. We never regretted it, but I was not fully satisfied in my own mind because Cáit was the name I always wanted, for no other reason than the drowning off the White Strand and in memory of our own Cáit, now dead many a long year. So Cáit had to be the name of the second child and that's what she was christened.

We were ploughing ahead and not finding it too much of a struggle. We had fishing every day of the year during the war and immediately after, and so far as good weather goes, we had that too. But when the war was over, the foreign trawlers began to appear off the coast again. There was a demand for fish on the English market and this put an end to fishing by currach. When the market for cured fish had closed in the States, it was the beginning of the end for mackerel fishing in winter. We now had to turn our hands to something else.

We found casual work on the roads and so on, but we were no longer as well off as we used to be when the fishing was thriving.

We had the lobster fishing every summer but, unless the weather was good, you had no great catch. All the same it only took a few of them to provide your pay, for they were fetching around ten pounds a dozen. On a really fine day you could have up to three dozen lobsters, but you had to work your shoulders and row some way from home in your search. In favourable weather you could be out from four in the morning

* Daughter of Máire Kennedy, the editor of Peig Sayers' books.

until nine at night. This was occasional only. When the weather changed we would have to stow our gear safely away, or we would find ourselves unprepared when it cleared once more.

After spending the whole of one day of good weather at the lobster pots, for little gain, we returned to find a man called Kennedy waiting for us at the harbour with a strange rambling tale to tell. It seemed that a man from the BBC was seeking to find four men from the barony who would undertake to make the voyage from Wexford across to Fishguard by currach. We took little interest at first in what he had to say for, when we heard him out and realized what a long journey was involved, we had little thought or notion in our heads of undertaking it.

There was another fellow who had not come in from the sea yet, and Kennedy was waiting to hear what he would say to it. He took us into the 'Well' and we had a couple of tots of whiskey, and a couple more. As these were taking effect, the blood began to warm up inside us and the courage to rise; the 'red woman' was producing a change of tune. What put the crown on it was hearing how much money we could make by the voyage. It was how we couldn't wait then to set out.

At last Tomás came in from the sea and, as soon as he arrived and heard all about the big money, he nearly tore the house down.

'It doesn't matter in the devil to me,' he said, 'so long as I have the Islandmen with me.'

One of the proposed crew was a middle-aged man who blew hot and cold all the while, unable to make up his mind.

'From Ireland to England,' he declared, 'I'd have to have the *Queen Mary* to tackle it. Certainly not this cockleshell of a currach!'

There was no persuading him but, when he had drink taken, there was no holding him and no hero in the west like him. When the drop had gone cold he would declare the whole affair was insanity and that anyone taking it on was fit for the madhouse. That was the crack and that was the sport. But on the day when the motor came to fetch us, it was God's will that he had the courage of the bottle again. He jumped in and came along with us. And he did a man's share, you can be sure, better than some of us, maybe, that had been raring to go. We made the voyage and came safe home, but the account of it would fill another book, if someone had the will and the time to write it.

Work started on the roads when we came home after our journey. It was a big scheme to last for as long as five or six years, and men drawing the dole had the first claim to a job. As luck would have it I was called to join the scramble, and a lorry came along on the Monday morning to take a load of us off to the quarry at Ventry. And what work! Breaking and splitting stones we were from morning to night with crowbars and sledge-hammers. I promise you that the cake of bread earned at the quarry was bread hard earned.

But, after putting the first month in, the work came easier to us than we expected. We grew used to the way of it though to some of us it was foreign entirely. The lobster and other fishing were over now and, I own to you, even during the summer months we would rather have crowbar and sledge than be putting up with all the hardship over the lobster pot. It is often indeed you would not have a halfpenny to show for it, after a week tending the lobster pots, if the sea was not calm. We were taking the new work in our stride after the first couple of months.

Then people began saying it wasn't right to have the same men wielding the sledge day after day and month after month. It was hard work, so they should be given something else to do while others took their place. The ganger raised it with the engineer and the answer he got was that, for his part, he was well pleased with the men on the sledge and, says he, 'if you put others in their place they won't be nearly as good.'

We were left on the sledge-hammer from then on and it was all equal to us what job we did with it so long as we had it in our hands. We would not have given it up even if we were asked.

This work lasted for a number of years and it was good to have. It was a form of assistance the Government gave to the people of the locality since the fishing had failed entirely, and they depending on it for their sole means of livelihood. If you had to be laid off, and you had the correct number of stamps put up, you would have a long full half-year drawing more than half your pay. If this happened during the summer we would have the lobster into the bargain which was better again. With stamp and lobster we were on the pig's back and we having the life of the dung-beetle.

It was seldom now you would hear any of us saying, 'It would be good to be back on the Island.' It was very rarely this tune was heard except when someone would strike up for no other reason than to set someone else going. For, my woe and the sorrows of my heart! We had learnt it was far apart the two places were. That's not to say the Blasket would not crop up naturally at other times when we would be reminiscing about the old pursuits and events of our youth. Something that had happened to this one or that. When did Peaid die or Máire Eoin; when did the five asses fall down the cliff? This was only for the crack, if we were short of something to talk about. We did not have that here, for we had no knowledge of the place or what the people were like until we came to settle here. It is back on the Island our books of knowledge used to be and they are the books we read still.

Before I finish my story I would say that I am duty bound before God and in fairness to mention here the noble people of

Dunquin. But for them, no Christian could ever have lived on the Blasket. It was the people of Dunquin that came to our rescue on the day of our need and they didn't begrudge it. There they were, ready with horse and cart whenever we wanted them. When we found ourselves stormbound and unable to make it back to our own cabins, there was bed and board for us in the houses of Dunquin and a welcome to share whatever food they had themselves.

As an old saying has it, 'The Islander has to repay the man on the mainland.'

The world knows that the Dunquin man could not be dancing attendance on you, for ever and always, without some reward for his pains but, the way things were in those days, it was the small recompense. Trouble galore and late hours he had to put up with, for we were headstrong and awkward whenever we had the drop of drink on board.

Most of the folk who gave us hospitality in those days have gone on the road of truth by now, and most of the Islanders likewise. So, I have no other means or way of expressing my thanks to them here except only to ask the God of bright Glory to grant their souls the pleasure and joy of heaven.

The years are not long passing when a person has the health and no grounds for complaint. We had no cause to complain from the day we set foot on the patch we have here still. We were independent ever. That was something we inherited, for our family before us relied on their own resources and I was the only one left to carry on the tradition. It stood me in good stead always to break the ice and to hold my head up too.

Our eldest daughter Niamh came of age and hoisted sail for America. She spent five years there, came home and went off again. After another couple of years she was back home to us once more and, before we knew where we were, she was married to a local lad and was comfortably settled on our doorstep. It was a great ease to our minds that she was back in her own country once more and so near to us, banishing all worries over the place across the ocean.

Cáit was grown up too and had gone to a college in Dublin. Seven years she spent there, going and coming, until she qualified as a domestic science teacher. Now she lives in Dingle, teaching in the technical school there.

While all this was going on, the years of our lives were speeding by and, before we knew it, old age was knocking at the door but, truth to tell, if it was, we did not feel old. I would dance a step yet, and I do when the fish are rising, as boldly as any man. There is no night indeed that gives a greater lift to my old heart than one that gives me the chance. People would say, I suppose, that it is doting I am. But dancing keeps me young and what does it matter to me so long as it does that?

Old age will give everyone no more than his due and I dare say nobody should make himself out to be young. There are people, though, who do not admit to themselves that they have ploughed out to the end of their furrow until they get there. A man's wits wander a little when he reaches a certain age. Maybe this is a great boon bestowed upon him towards the latter end of his days and I expect it to happen to me too if I am spared.

To reach pension age was regarded as quite a good age in days gone by. But, like everything else in the modern world, nobody says so or thinks so today. Still, for everyone that reaches it, there are many more who do not. A few may even reach the four score years of the priest, but again compare this to all that are dead and gone and what does it come to?

We have had our day. It is toiling on the sea I have spent most of my life. You have a chance of coming home safe if you keep your weather eye open and can read the signs.

My wife and I have grown old together. Neither of us was

looking for a divorce, nor did we know down the years that there was such a thing. When the great squalls raged and a thousand words were only like a dozen to her, all I could do was pay out the rope and leave it slack. I knew she would not carry away any of my nets. If I spoke I was done for, because she had a head seven times better than my own.

We carry on in the same old way still, thanks be to God, and isn't strife better than loneliness? When a man is a pensioner and has that stamped across his forehead, there's no end to the remarks thrown in your face: 'Your wits are going astray!' 'You have the disease, boy!' 'If you live long more who will stand you?' And so on. The stamp of the pensioner is on me now and I am a *jaingléir* like the rest. And if there is any other stamp to come it can't be far off.

But of all the stamps none is more sure and certain than that of the Man with the Staff. He puts on his own stamp and takes no account of any that was there before. We shall all have to travel the same road as those who travelled it before us. May the God of bright Glory grant all who will read these pages after me a proper preparation for death, and joy in the boat of Paradise among the saints and angels!